S

D0779510

EXPOSED BY THE MASK

EXPOSED BY THE MASK

Form and Language in Drama

PETER HALL

THEATRE COMMUNICATIONS GROUP

TEXAS WOMAN'S UNIVERSITY LIBRARY

Copyright © 2000 by Peter Hall

Exposed by the Mask is published by
Theatre Communications Group, Inc.,
355 Lexington Avenue, New York, NY 10017-6603
by special arrangement with Oberon Books, Ltd.

All rights reserved. Except for brief passages quoted in newspaper, magazine, radio or television reviews, no part of this book may be reproduced in any form or by any means, electronic or mechanical, including photocopying or recording, or by an information storage or retrieval system, without permission in writing from the publisher.

Extracts from *The Theatrical Notebooks of Samuel Beckett—Waiting for Godot* and *The Homecoming* by Harold Pinter, reprinted by kind permission of Grove/Atlantic Press.

CIP catalog information for this book is available from the Library of Congress.

This publication is made possible in part with public funds from the New York State Council on the Arts, a State Agency.

TCG Books are exclusively distributed to the book trade by Consortium Book Sales and Distribution, 1045 Westgate Dr., St. Paul, MN 55114.

Cover design: by Paton Walker
On the Cover: Masks by Vicki Hallam for *Lenny,*
photograph by Martin Allen

First TCG edition, September 2000

To Nicki

CONTENTS

Preface

I must thank Trinity College Cambridge for asking me to do the prestigious Clark Lectures and thus forcing me to think about what was special to the theatre in the past and what might be special in the future.

Directors spend their lives talking in rehearsal rooms: perhaps we are all given to talking too much. As a consequence, I have recklessly given lectures all my life by thinking on my feet. I love public speaking. I have always found it more interesting to see someone trying to define their thoughts rather than merely repeating them from a typed script. But the Clark Lectures were different. They had to be published, and as they were to be (partly) available on the internet, because the lectures were to be filmed. There was also the problem of repeating myself, since all four lectures were aimed at the same target and yet were given at weekly intervals.

So I wrote them, but I wrote them for speaking. It seemed right to leave the text in its original form and let them be seen in print as they were delivered. I hope the reader will therefore forgive my colloquial exuberance and my quirky grammar and constructions.

My central concern was that plays and opera scores should be studied as live drama and not as a collection of words and images, or a sequence of notes and phrases. My allegation that the ancient universities were still reluctant to study plays as plays aroused irritation in some of those who teach there. But students still tell me that too much of the time studying plays is devoted to thought and image and not enough to the reasons why a play is a play and works as a play. It is like studying music without having heard a note of it – or being unable to "hear" the music of a score as you read it.

I don't for a minute think that Oxford or Cambridge should have drama departments or award degrees in drama. Cambridge particularly has dominated the professional theatre for the last fifty years precisely because of the creative chaos of its amateur theatre, and the consequent unrivalled opportunities it offers to find out by doing. The students – and I was one – untrammelled by the interference of teachers or the constrictions of syllabus or exams, find out how to survive in the theatre. So I am not concerned about those who seek to be professionals. But the majority, who are studying drama (surely the biggest humanist treasure chest in the west), should have greater help in understanding that it is never literature.

I wish to thank the Master and Fellows of Trinity College, Cambridge for their welcome and their hospitality; Professor Anne Barton for her support and graciousness; and my ever-enthusiastic publisher, James Hogan. I thank also Corinne Beaver, my assistant, who typed my dictated and then corrected thoughts over and over until she must have been sick of them.

Peter Hall
London, 2000

THE GREEKS

The Greeks

It is a blessing to me (since I inhabit to some extent both their worlds) that theatre people and academics now often talk the same language. It was not so fifty years ago.

They still both, of course, have their extreme positions. Concept theatre (where the director of a Shakespeare play tells the actors what the production is to say before the company have actually had a chance to find out what the play actually says) is as uncreative as the deconstructionist antics of minor Shakespearean scholarship. They both contrive to destroy the marvel of Shakespeare, denigrate his particularity, and forget that his plays were made to be performed. As a consequence, his theatre always celebrates the ambiguous and the contradictory: it is rich, not simple. It is no place for either dogmatic directors or theorists.

The plays of the past and the plays of the present are well studied in our society. But they are still largely dissected as linguistic evidence, as though they were poems – or used as theatre exercises by people who are training to be actors. These are the two extremes: plays are either seen as literature – or used as the raw material of performance. In either case, there is little understanding of what an audience does to them and how essential an audience – and the need to share them with an audience – is to their meaning.

The same is true of opera. The play exists as a text; opera as a score. But without performance of both, their meaning is evidently incomplete, expressing only a part – albeit the beginning part – of their creator's meaning. Drama should be performed – or at the very least the nature of its live performance must be understood by those who are studying it.

I am not here either to advance the cause of drama departments or of drama schools. But I still cannot understand how our two ancient universities for the most part study drama with no tradition of considering plays as <u>plays</u>. By looking at them only as texts, they are constantly in danger of simplifying them. Novels have the interpretative certainty of the authorial voice, telling us how to hear the dialogue. Poems benefit by the controlling presence of the poet's sensibility. But a dramatic text is much more ambiguous – and much more at a distance from its creator: his words are making dialogue for other people. We must add to these words an understanding of how they operate when spoken aloud, and what their form, shape and rhythm contribute to the emotional meaning of the character who is speaking them. We must also be aware of what the dramatist was asking of the actor – indeed almost what <u>kind</u> of acting is indicated by the text. For it must be imagined in living terms.

We also need some knowledge of the stage that the play was written for and how it operated, plus a consideration of the original audience, its preoccupations and its sensibilities. All this will help us read the text of the play as a living experience. Above all, an understanding of the drama's form always helps release the writer's intentions.

Aristotle defined the parts of drama in a significant order. He specified: PLOT, CHARACTER, LANGUAGE, THOUGHT, THE VISUAL, MUSIC. Plot is first. Well is it plot? It is the vexed word MUTHOS: vexed because it is one of those portmanteau Greek words which means a multitude of things – story, narrative, myth, theme, communication of an emotionally charged representation of men acting or being acted upon and experiencing as a consequence success or defeat.

Characters enact plot and communicate it. And they do so by the use of dramatic language (words, thought, visuals, music). These means of expression are what I define as form. But since the beginning and end of theatre is the plot, the form functions primarily as narrative.

In these four lectures, I will examine how practical work on form has helped my understanding – first of the Greeks; then of Shakespeare's verse; and then the dramatic techniques of Mozart's operas. I shall finish with some of the images of Beckett and Pinter, for they have both made the theatre a place rich in metaphor again. I have picked these four subjects out of a lifetime of work because they illustrate vividly that great drama is much less than itself if it is divorced from its stage.

Let us first, as any healthy society must, listen to our clowns. A great American comic – George Burns – once said:

The most important thing about acting is honesty.
If you can fake that, you have got it made.

Don't be deceived. This is a profound remark. We all know that any performance – any piece of theatre, whether it be opera, or ballet, or play is in fact totally unreal. It portrays simulated actions and simulated emotions. It pretends to be that which it is not. Yet we people of the theatre who spend our lives trying to create these fictions, judge them by evaluating their "truth". "He is a very <u>true</u> actor." "The performance is <u>true</u> to life." A praised production is <u>convincing</u> and is an evening filled with <u>reality</u>, though we manipulate the audience in the hope that they will forget where they are and who we are.

In fact nothing is real at all except the actors, the audience and the theatre in which they sit. And the audience and the theatre people all know that we are dealing with simulation. If what is on stage is intense enough, it will provoke and support the imagination of the audience so that they pretend that what is said is what <u>is</u>. Yet however intense the experience, those on stage and those in the audience never, I believe, forget that they are in a theatre. Dr Johnson's bracing words always reassure me as I begin the series of deceptions that make up any act of theatre:

> The truth is, that the spectators are always in their senses, and know, from the first act to the last, that the stage is only a stage, and that the players are only players.

What therefore, is theatrical truth? It is clearly not the same as the truth of everyday life. The actor is asked to pretend – to simulate – many things which he may know about: love, anger, jealousy, happiness, merriment. Yet he is also asked to simulate death. Now whatever any of us may know about life, we certainly know nothing whatever about death. Yet if the actor expires sensibly, with a correct degree of understatement and with a correct degree of "truth", we will be moved (though probably only for a short moment) almost as much as we would if we were faced with the reality of death. Yet in the theatre, because it is unreal, there is always restraint in this true reaction. There is temperance both in audience and actor – a temperance indeed "that may give it smoothness" – a quotation, for the first of many times, from *Hamlet*. Both actor and audience experience the emotion, but remain – as they might not in life – in control. Lack of control never produces art; and lack of control is never capable of appreciating art. Emotion in art needs tranquillity.

The fable must be credible because we must believe that it is a good deception. All the words in the theatre that define truth are of course expressing a central paradox: we are watching something that is not true at all, and we know it. The actor is always pretending. The stage is not reality, but a metaphor and the words are predetermined by the playwright. But an audience's praise is for the intensity of the deception. If it is acute enough, their imaginations will be fulfilled and they will have a satisfying evening. This is a sensitive and intricate contract and when it is broken there is acute disappointment, even anger. A bad film irritates or provokes the giggles. A bad performance with live actors appals and embarrasses. An audience feels foolish if the performance is not sensible and they cannot believe in it. Perhaps this is why theatre is the only art whose technical terms are regularly used as metaphors of abuse. We dislike somebody who lives his life "dramatically". To be "theatrical" is a pejorative description. To "go over the top" is a demonstration of emotional dishonesty. Perhaps all this is a compliment to the theatre. Because the audience knows how good theatre can be, they bitterly resent it when it is bad.

To create a suspension of disbelief is the task that drives everybody in the theatre. Yet the agreement with the audience is made from complicity rather than confrontation. The audience like to know how it is done. True theatre does not finally deceive: we see and acknowledge how it is done and that it is part of a game of make-believe. A great conjurer or magician deceives an audience almost to the point of mockery, and there is an element of the challenge in his attitude to them. But magic of this kind quickly becomes boring – if you can materialise a gleaming Rolls-Royce with four white leopards in it out of thin air (as the celebrated illusionists Siegfried and Roy do in Las Vegas) there are clearly no more surprises: anything is possible. True theatre only deceives to a point: like children we want to see and acknowledge how it is done, while agreeing to ignore this knowledge. It is part of the great game of make-believe. In Monteverdi's baroque opera *Il Ritorno D'Ulisse*, the goddess Athena hovers above the journeying Ulysses as a caring presence. When he finally arrives in Ithica, Athena descends from the clouds and, as she touches the earth, instantaneously turns into a shepherd boy. There is precisely no time in the music to effect this change. The great designer, John Bury, understood the make-believe of this moment and that the audience would want to be a part of it. Athena was dressed as a shepherd boy, but stood on a stirrup flying high above the stage. Built on to the stirrup was a breastplate, a goddess' skirt, a helmet, and a spear. Athena stood inside it, her face showing below the helmet. When the stirrup touched the ground, Athena simply walked out of the armour and revealed what she had been wearing underneath: a shepherd boy's smock. The audience knew how it was done, yet they gasped every night.

The pleasure of believing is part of playing, especially when you know how it is done. Children get very angry with any other child in the group who will not maintain the group fantasy.

Children play in order to learn. They need no encouragement to improvise, dress-up, and become things they are not. They have a concentration – and thus a belief – which is absolute. The only sin is to break the concentration by not believing – by not playing. Anyone who breaks the spell, who fails to believe, is ostracised. Yet their play is not all good, all happy. The imaginings can often take them to the darker side of life. Fear is part of play: it can be terrifying.

It is a long step from this play to performances for others to watch. Children play for themselves, not for others. It is therapy rather than art. To turn such improvisations into drama will need economy, selection and the discipline of form. Above all, it will need a story. A story can shape raw emotion into art. Play becomes a <u>Play</u> – something that spectators can react to, even learn from. Let us therefore never forget the deep instinctual need to make drama, or the psychic and emotional health of this activity. Whether we are children or adults, we can through play, escape to a new reality – and this is both for those who perform, and those who are performed to.

Where do we play? For centuries we have played in a public place, a theatre – literally a place for viewing or, as the Greeks would have it, a place where we "look at". It is a glass that enables us to magnify and scrutinise the emotions. But we also need, as David Hare has said, "a slight touch of distance if we are going to be able to think and feel at the same time. That distance, naturally, is provided by form". We magnify, but we also objectify.

And without form – in language, action and presentation, we remain in the realms of therapy. We have not art but anarchy. Only by the limitation of form can we express the limitless. And it is this tension between freedom and form, between creativity and discipline where the flash-point of drama occurs that enables us to see and feel and understand beyond our individual limitations. An audience is always more intelligent than its individual members. There is the mysterious and instinctive side to drama – something which values words, but is beyond words. It is partly the magnetism of the actor, the heart-stopping illumination that the spoken metaphor can give a listener; or the sudden shifting cadences in the overture of *Don Giovanni.*

> Many wise men and great philosophers have thought the theatre to the mind <u>as the bow to the fiddle</u>; and certain it is, though a great secret in nature, that the minds of men in company are more open to affections and impressions than when alone.

This is Francis Bacon. He believed what is more that theatre "might improve mankind in virtue", and having given drama a moral purpose (for what play, however alarming, however violent has ever actually encouraged vice?) tries to define the ancient mystery of public communication. Theatre is a live contract: at each performance, the audience agrees to imagine with the actor. The contract is sealed by the form. It is form that makes the high emotions acceptable or the complex arguments understandable. The form is the style, the metre, the music, the alliteration, the metaphors, the economy – it selects from human reality and gives it shape. It makes art. It makes drama.

"Drama" for the Greeks meant to do, to act, or to perform. From its beginnings it meant character in action, conflict that engendered emotion, in actor and in spectator. The earliest form is the story – with its beginning, middle and end. The voices of the storytellers – the Bards – passed on orally the great, inherited stories from generation to generation and from tribe to tribe. The early creation myths have strange similarities. Is it the response to similar circumstances? Or the sharing of narrative models? Both, probably.

But out of all the welter of speculation about Homer – whether he was one or many, whether his great epics were a patchwork sewn together of ancient ballads, or a renovation of old material, one thing is certain about the *Iliad* and the *Odyssey*: the stories are told in a language that no one ever spoke. It is an artificial, poetic language, brim full of archaisms, incongruities, and inventions. The language of Homer is deliberately one that nobody, except poets or priests (both of whom, like dramatists, try to make us think and feel at the same time) would ever dream of using. The language is formalised to make drama.

> Sing in me Muse, and through me tell the story
> of that man skilled in all ways of contending,
> the wanderer, harried for years on end,
> after he plundered the strong hold
> on the proud height of Troy.

That is Robert Fitzgerald's translation, setting the stage and setting the scene. We are now ready for drama. The form – the invocation – is intended to take us up to a level where mighty emotions and mighty conflicts can be expressed. The stuff of these epics became, many centuries later, the raw material for the first great period of drama that survives: the Greek. The myths were interpreted, reinterpreted, and contradicted. And they have gone on being reinterpreted for nearly three thousand years. A myth cannot be ancient: it lives because it is still potent – it speaks to us. In that sense, it remains modern by definition; otherwise, it would not be audible. It would not have survived.

Theatre and myth helps us to understand the mysteries of life – birth and desire, love and death, revenge and forgiveness. And the Greek theatre began the task of representing them. They always have been and always will be the stuff of theatre – the stuff of the actor's art. And every age must re-examine them because of our desperate need to understand.

Here is a very interesting paradox. Any actor will tell you that if you wish to move an audience, you must not cry. Do <u>not</u> cry. If you cry, the audience will not. The actor must exercise restraint. It is made easier for him if the form provides a mask – the emotion can then be expressed without indulgence. Ophelia's outburst, "Oh what a noble mind is here o'er thrown!" after the Nunnery scene, expresses the girl's complete breakdown. The level of tearful emotion is such that if the actress allows it to be "real", the speech is incomprehensible. It is also impossible to believe that a girl gripped by such hysteria would invent the rhetorical cadences that balance so perfectly, and express her regrets in what is in effect a sonnet. The verse is here indeed a kind of mask. It enables Ophelia to contain and govern her emotions, so that she can describe the consequences of them rather than indulge them. The form is the conductor of her emotions; and for the actress, it both induces it and disciplines it.

A child who comes towards you trying <u>not</u> to cry (but who is filled with suppressed tears) is incredibly moving. But a child crying his heart out, a child in extremis, is less certain of our acceptance. There is something naturally repulsive about grief – particularly extreme grief. The actor is in the same situation. The paradox is that drama deals with huge emotions; but if it displays them in a hugely emotional way, in indulgent terms, the audience is liable to reject them. They are unpleasant, unbelievable, even repulsive. To be acceptable on the stage, they must be stage-real – which means transformed, shaped and contained.

The Greeks, of course, knew how to deal with this. They knew that their society needed to experience extreme tragedy and wild anarchic comedy in order to remain sane. Drama allowed them the objectivity of art, the distance that allows us to study something while experiencing it. Hence the mask.

In Greek tragedy, the bloodiest actions are kept off the stage. Similarly, the most hysterical behaviour is contained by the mask. Both are disciplines of form. The audience is able to experience passions at an intensity which takes them beyond the moment of repulsion. The screaming, naked, human face would repel. The face of the mask – with the scream behind it – does not. A great mask indeed has no expression. It is ambiguous. The sound of a scream presented as part of the body language of hysteria makes the mask scream. The sound of ribald laughter makes the mask laugh.

The Greek stage itself – keeping all fundamental or violent action off stage – is a mask. It is a platform with double doors. Behind those doors, lies the horror, that which is mythical. Behind those doors the unexpected can and does happen. Whatever its horror, it is unseen, imagined. It would be diminished in power if it came on stage. The bodies of Agamemnon and Clytemnestra are shown after we have heard their screams and imagined their deaths. In front of the platform for the principals is the arena where the Chorus sing and dance and tell the story. They are our representatives, our interpreters. They ask our questions, propose our answers. They too are masked.

Throughout its history the Greek theatre remained masked. A few actors represented many principal characters by donning many masks. All ancient drama, whether it be the rain dances of the American Indians, or the epic story-tellings of the East that try to define the gods, all used masks. Why?

We moderns are very patronising about masks. We pretend that primitive societies wore masks because they were so undeveloped, so unsophisticated emotionally, that the only way they could make drama was by putting on something that was a caricature of humanity. Of course, this cannot be true. They could have used their faces: they had them. But they did not want to use their faces. They wanted to use a mask. Why?

I think it is in every case an attempt to know the unknowable, to experience the unspeakable and to enact the repulsive. The mask enables the audience to contemplate a passion at an intensity which goes beyond the moment of rejection.

I am therefore led to believe that performance always has to have the equivalent of a mask in order to transmit an emotion. It must have a mask, even if it is not a literal mask. It needs the equivalent if it is to deal with primal passions. It demands form – either in its text, or its physical life, or its music. All these can act like a Greek mask. Only then can strong feeling be dealt with.

We can develop this thought so that we regard the form of the stage itself as a mask. The dramatist, by creating the shape of his text (in Shakespeare's case, the intricate tension of his blank verse) is making a mask that enables him to express and yet contain high passion. I have said that you cannot play Shakespeare in tears. Similarly, you cannot play an angry speech of Shakespeare's angrily. You might get through a line or two in anger; but then you would find you could not "think" the antitheses or the alliteration or the balance of the iambics. You could not, indeed, communicate the actual sense. Suppose a character in Shakespeare is angry. So he <u>talks</u> about anger, invents metaphors of anger at that moment to describe his state. He may need to feel anger inside him, but he can never indulge that anger by letting it out. He must contain it and express it through the rational and descriptive form of the verse. At that moment the verse disciplines the feeling in much the same way as the Greek mask disciplines the body.

Any defined form in the theatre performs as a mask: it releases rather than hides; it enables emotion to be specific rather than generalised. It permits control while it prevents indulgence. Form frees, it does not inhibit. And the mask – whether it be the physical mask of the Greek theatre, the mask of Shakespeare's verse, the underlying formal grammar of Mozart's music, or the personal cadences of Tennessee Williams or Samuel Beckett – is always <u>telling</u> us about the emotion rather than parading it. Wilde's mask is his wit. His characters make up epigrams as a kind of stiff-upper-lip activity to govern and hide their deep emotional moments. Their epigrams are a way of getting through stress. The subtext of *An Ideal Husband* or even of *The Importance of Being Ernest* is often violently emotional; and it is what humanises an apparently artificial text.

Throughout history, all art forms have renewed themselves by challenging and questioning accepted form. So theatre always flirts with taboos, moral, ethical and political. After the Greeks many later dramas insisted on performing dangerously. There are constant attempts through the centuries to revitalise the form by flirting with the unexpected. Theatre cannot help shocking because it is part of its need to challenge an audience to investigate the extremes of life. So Gloucester is blinded on stage. And Titus Andronicus cuts his hand off.

It is of course a pretence. We would not be moved if Titus really cut his hand off. We would be horrified and the theatre would speedily be closed. We all know that we are playing a game of make-believe. But the play has to be true. And the form has to encourage our objectivity. Belief in "play" is what the theatre lives on. And by means of play, we are enabled to imagine that one pillar represents the whole of Ancient Rome. It also enables an actress with the objectivity of someone in their late twenties to tell us what it is like to be a fourteen-year-old Juliet. On film, she has to be fourteen, for the camera demands reality. On stage, we will prefer the older actress. She can tell us more about being fourteen.

❖

I have done Greek plays in ancient Greek theatres and have been forced to contemplate techniques which I have never thought of in the study or found in a book.

First, the mask. At once, the baroque image comes to mind – two masks looking to left and right, one contorted with laughter, the other afflicted with grief. Comedy and tragedy. The contradiction is eloquent – and decorative, for this is an emblem of the baroque, and the influence is Roman, not Greek. The Romans believed in absolutes: so their masks were good or bad, serious or comic. "Is he a goodie or a baddie?" says the child, seeking reassurance. So said the Romans because they wanted absolutes, not, like the Greeks, questions. The Greek mask was enigmatic, uncertain, representing the human confusion. They were soft, flexible, probably made of thin leather, and always ambiguous. Their humanity was enigmatic. They waited to be printed with the emotion of the actor. So they were neither comic nor tragic – like life itself. The Romans always needed the reassurance of caricature. Greek masks are on a human scale; Roman masks are gargantuan.

A Greek full mask can laugh or cry – it is entirely dependent on what the character wearing it is feeling. This can be as well expressed by the body as by the words that are uttered. The ambiguous mask, fully used, is often much more expressive than the human face because it is dealing with the quintessence of emotions. Its contradictions and yet its simplicity enable a range of feeling and an extremity of passion to be expressed which is often much more difficult with a naked face. The mask is an instrument of communication. The poet Tony Harrison sees it as the incandescent spot of the welder's torch, where meaning is fused and components joined. Or it can be thought of as a magnifying glass, helping us to scrutinise emotion. Uneasy attempts to explain it away are partly modern embarrassment when faced with primal feelings – or bad mask work where the passions are not strong enough to support the form. Then abstraction sets in and the mask appears dead.

The mask is <u>not</u> a device to enhance visibility in the large Greek amphitheatres; a mask of human scale is perfectly visible in Epidaurus before ten thousand people. Nor is the mask a megaphone to increase audibility. Epidaurus has no need of megaphones – only of clear consonants expressing clear thoughts. Ten thousand people can hear perfectly.

With the governance of the mask preventing overacting and telling us about grief rather than realistically crying it out, it is entirely possible to make subtle drama at Epidaurus. Precise words and eloquent actions give a clear meaning, which is in no sense ritualised. Yet the masks enable an intense emotional heat to be generated that <u>tells</u> us about grief. The same is true of the comic mask. The surrealistic extremes of Aristophanes are perfectly acceptable in this world of caricature. Without the mask, his crudity can lack grace. It runs the risk of being not life-enhancing, but just plain dirty, like an obvious seaside postcard.

Above all, the mask is the tool of the imagination. A metaphor. An audience can see on it infinite emotions. A camera will only see an immobile mask. But the camera is literal – it has no imagination. Once the mask is accepted, the work with the actor, particularly the work with the Chorus, becomes very specific. And it is here that the discoveries are biggest.

I was taught (and I can hear) that the most complex pieces of writing in Aeschylus, Sophocles and Euripides are expressed by the Chorus. There we find the richest metaphors, the most intricate paradoxes, and the most haunting lyrics.

The Choruses of Greek tragedy express a highly complicated form of verbal theatre. So how were they performed? Danced? Only surely as a secondary action to the words. Eloquent movement destroys eloquent words:

> Those in motion sooner catch the eye
> Than what not moves.

Some say they were sung. I don't believe it. The sung text can never be a complex text. An audience simply can't understand sung words unless they are extraordinarily simple. Ambiguity comes from the inevitable tension between the music and the words, not from trying to unpack the complexity of the words themselves as you struggle to distinguish them. Sung words are never easily understandable. They inform the performer so that he can induce an emotion. But those same words are rarely communicated in full to the listener. The feeling, yes; verbal intricacy, no. Sur-titles have given a new dimension to opera in the last twenty years. But if we are honest, it is not just understanding in a foreign language that is difficult. Eighty per cent of the time, we cannot understand opera in English either. Anything heavier than the delicate orchestration of Monteverdi (where the word is always primary) and it becomes virtually impossible to understand a complex text with an orchestra playing. We now indeed use sur-titles for English operas as well.

Other solutions are advanced for the Chorus. We know that the dramatists "drilled" or rehearsed the Choruses for the entire year before the dramatic competitions. That was his task and he paid for it; or raised sponsorship to pay for it. Some believe that this resulted in an awesome uniformity, so that the text was spoken meticulously – rather like the equivalent of a group of verbal Tiller Girls, lifted inflections like precisely lifted limbs. But even if choral speaking is well drilled so that every syllable is precisely in unison, the very efficiency produces a dehumanising effect, and is certainly no aid either to understanding or to the provocation of the listener's imagination. Uniform speech is like uniform movement: abstract and inhuman. It does not provoke feeling.

So how were the Choruses performed? I believe that a single voice either spoke or sung or chanted every line that was complex. It could then be understood.

Let me explain: fifteen old men of Argos appear to argue, contradict each other and then draw conclusions from their opinions. Then they question them again. There seems no unanimity in this community. Yet unanimity – or rather, fleeting agreements, changing like light on water – is what the Greek Chorus is all about. They stand in the orchestra, often as the representatives of us, the audience, speaking to the protagonists, who are on the upper stage. Those protagonists – the leading actors – never speak to the audience. Their dialogue is exclusively with the Chorus, who then turn and talk to us. They comment on their findings and interpret the protagonists to us.

I believe this is how the Choruses were performed: when fifteen old men of Argos all wear the same configuration of full mask, they are fifteen old men who are united in age, race and attitude. But because the actors are all different, with subtly different body language, the masks, though the same, will all look slightly different. Yet they will also look sufficiently the same to be a collective. There is a reassuring similarity, but not an arid uniformity.

Now, if one voice says a line and the other fourteen act the line, it appears that they have all spoken it. With a full mask, it is impossible to know who has spoken because no lips move. So all the masks appear to create the line that only one voice utters. The most complex line is therefore understandable. The lines are shared out between the fifteen; one voice proposes, one voice opposes; one voice develops the meaning, another qualifies it. All the Chorus learn the full text, and act the full text, even when not speaking.

I do not believe a Greek Chorus argues with itself – or that it denies itself. Say rather that it vacillates as one person might as their thoughts run on a subject. What is proposed one moment may well be opposed the next. What is affirmed, can often be denied. The Chorus expresses in a modern, psychological sense, the ebb and flow of doubt and belief, of resolution and irresolution in each individual's thoughts. If we are honest, our opinions are changed and modified by the second as they rush round our heads like a flock of uncertain sheep. The Chorus can suddenly shout as one, or cry as one when the emotion is hot – and therefore simple and straightforward. At that instant, the words can be straightforward too. They can also sing as one when the intensity of emotion lifts them into making music. But the complex arguments are created by the subconscious of the group and uttered by the single voice. Before Jung or Freud, before Joyce or Beckett, the stream of consciousness was on the stage.

Movement works in a very similar way if the discipline of the mask is respected. Moods are expressed by the sudden body reactions of the group as the impulse to move is passed from one to another. The Chorus behave like a shoal of fish or a flock of starlings. A movement develops from an individual and is passed through the group. It may grow into a rush of panic, or simply subside into an ominous stillness. Over all this, the mask presides, concentrating our attention. It not only allows extremes of emotion; it allows the moods of a group to change like lightning.

For the actor, the mask asserts another need: if he is part of the Chorus, he must present himself to the audience or to the protagonist (when he will have his back to the audience). If he is a protagonist, he must always present his mask out-front to the Chorus. The mask goes dead in profile. It is always the full face that expresses what the heart is feeling. The whole body endorses that feeling when it moves or dances. Full masks do not look at each other. To see another masked figure close to you, shatters the inward illusion, the belief in another person that the actor is creating for himself. The mask is therefore always "presented" to the audience, telling the story of the character. In a sense, each actor in a masked play is an individual on his own.

Much of this is, of course, profoundly unfashionable. The individual may be freed by the mask, but in an individualistic society, the actor naturally wants to be himself and express himself. In a Chorus, he is part of a complex group and can feel obscured by a mask. But the work can in fact end up as a liberation rather than a constriction. The human choices the actor can make – the emotional choices he can follow – are infinite. By accepting the form, accepting the mask – whether it be a musical discipline, or iambic pentameters, or intricate dance steps – the actor is finally freed to use all of himself. The mask becomes him.

❖

It is worth considering the technique of the full mask in greater detail. A variety of masks and hats with odd bits of clothes and pieces of material are spread out on a table. The actors are asked to take any mask, any item of clothing that appeals to their imaginations and dress themselves up to make a character. There is now a traumatic moment. The actor looks for the first time into a full-length mirror. He or she must then <u>become</u> what they see. Become the character. So the look lasts for a few seconds. No more. Just a few seconds. The changed identity is then accepted by the actor and the character now follows the change wherever it may lead.

Sometimes the actor is so alarmed by the new self that he rejects it. Then he must take the mask off – immediately. He must also take it off if he feels untrue. Even the least talented actor knows when he is being untrue to his character. But then he cannot go on wearing the mask. He must always be true to it.

Sometimes the mask liberates him. Sometimes it makes the actor apprehend a whole new world. He can change his age, his bearing, his physique, even his sexuality. The change comes from using parts of himself that perhaps he did not know existed, and suppressing others irrelevant to this new person. It is the same process as the creation of a realistic character, but the mask allows the actor a much, much wider range.

When the actor first puts on the mask, he finds it almost impossible to speak. If he works honestly, he goes through a period – and it can take sometimes two to three weeks – where all he can do is make guttural sounds. He ignores everyone. Or if he looks at them, he looks belligerently. Sometimes the shock of seeing others makes him remove the mask. Sometimes he sinks into a strange torpor. After a time, he gradually starts making sounds and words for himself. After finding his place in a social group, the hostility recedes and he begins to make sounds at others. After even more time, words may be exchanged.

This somewhat alarming process of growing up, of becoming part of a group and learning how to live in it has happened every single time I have conducted a mask workshop. On several occasions, the actors had no knowledge that our work would produce this journey. Yet it always went the same way. The actor always had to learn to speak and then to grow up. He had to take on social responsibilities, and as he did so he became less hostile. Every time, I observed the animal learning to be human. There are truly primitive forces at work here. And the mask can have alarming consequences. I have seen an actor arrested by a policeman when in full mask he exuberantly leapt on a bicycle and pedalled out of the rehearsal room into the Chelsea crowds. I have known an actor whose incipient nervous breakdown was hastened by contemplating himself in a mask.

In our post-Stanislavsky, screen-dominated age actors often worry about disciplines that can constrict their individuality. This is something that an opera singer, given the formal discipline of music, does not think twice about. It is actually impossible to sing Wagner or Puccini or even Mozart (I am not sure I should not say "especially" Mozart) unless you breathe in the right place. Only after the breathing is learnt can the performer start saying to himself, "What kind of person am I? What am I feeling in this situation? What am I trying to express?" The same is true of playing Shakespeare, Beckett, Pinter or Tennessee Williams – or any writer who communicates by the creation of a particular form.

So the actor has to endorse the form of any piece of drama. The Greek mask is an extreme example, but any form requires the actor to show the same abnegation of self and the same honesty.

I shall be considering the form of Shakespeare and the form of Mozart in subsequent lectures. There is a strange similarity in what, as artists, they inherited. Shakespeare received a formal tradition of English blank verse, of which Marlowe was the chief exponent. Mozart inherited the shape and architectural symmetry of baroque music. Shakespeare was thus able to take the regularity of the iambic pentameter, and by contradicting it with irregularities and cross-rhythms which almost (but not quite) destroy the form, make an infinitely expressive means to convey emotion. By the late plays, he is writing with a freedom that knows that his actors always have a regular iambic pentameter beating in their heads like the pulse of a jazz group. They can play with it or move against it, in order to express emotion, tension or confusion. By his maturity, Shakespeare could risk a blank verse line which is a complete inversion of the normal rhythm, but which he knows will express tragic agony because of its very formal contradiction:

Never. Never. Never. Never. Never.

Not:

NeVER. NeVER. NeVER. NeVER. NeVER.

Mozart, by his sudden shifts of key and experiments with chromaticism (which alarmed his contemporary audiences, though to us they express "real" anguish) was able to express a range of emotion almost unavailable to the composers before him. This was precisely because he was contradicting the formality he had been given.

The iambic pentameter is the mask of Shakespeare. The ensemble is the supreme mask of Mozart, the structure which allows his irony to be dramatic. Both of them, just like the masters of Greek drama, cannot begin to be interpreted without an appreciation of their form. Form contains the emotion and makes its expression acceptable. Hysteria is no longer indulgent, or action improbable. Without form there is no credibility, and no narrative. And so there is no involvement. And no drama.

SHAKESPEARE'S VERSE

Shakespeare's Verse

When I was making the Royal Shakespeare Company in the early 1960s, I received a letter which read:

Dear Mr Hall,

I am contemplating writing a book on the life and works of William Shakespeare and would be glad of any information that you could send me.

My correspondent little knew the size of the problem. I know it, as I contemplate surveying the form of Shakespeare in less than an hour.

To my mind, the form is still woefully neglected in the study of Shakespeare. Shakespeare's text tells an actor quite clearly when to go fast, when to go slow, when to pause, when to come in on cue. He indicates which word should be accented and which word should be thrown away. These are the results, the means of <u>expression</u> that the actor is left with at the end of reading the Shakespearean score. But Shakespeare never tells an actor <u>why</u> these are the results: that is the individual choice of the actor. He must decide what he must feel having studied the text.

Shakespeare's text is scored precisely. The actor's task is to engender a set of feelings which will make this textual shape, this end result, the true one. This brings us closer to Shakespeare's meaning than any other form of analysis that I know. Any student of Shakespeare is helped by it, not only the actor.

Yet there is little attention paid to the form of Shakespeare's verse in academic circles. And apart from John Barton's heroic theatre work with actors on both sides of the Atlantic (which sprung, as has my work, out of the early traditions of the Marlowe Society of this university, passed down to us by George Rylands), there is very little acceptance of a method of approaching verse in the professional theatre either. Most Shakespearean productions are a symphony of mis-scansions and mis-emphases and seem unaware of the fact. There are even misquotes – plain inaccuracies. We wouldn't accept wrong notes in Mozart.

Providing you are alert to the clues, all the dynamics of Shakespeare's verse are clearly marked. George Rylands initially taught me these clues at the Marlowe Society. The Society was founded in 1907, inspired by the example of William Poel, the great Shakespearean revolutionary and scourge of Irving. Poel brought Shakespeare back to a bare stage where the imagination could work more vividly than the scene painter. He also brought the text back to Hamlet's requirements, speaking it "trippingly on the tongue" – the state, he said that verse-speaking was in until Irving set the fashion of slow, sonorous speech. Poel's rapid, witty technique was learnt from the actors in Macready's company. He said they had been taught by Kean's actors, who had been taught by Garrick's, who had been taught by Betterton's. That was as far back as he could go. There the tradition petered out. The Puritans had destroyed it.

William Poel taught Harley Granville Barker, who played Richard II for him. (Incidentally, I believe

Barker is still the best commentator on Shakespeare's plays as plays.) Poel also directed as Cressida, the seventeen-year-old Edith Evans, fresh from her milliner's shop. She was one of the first great actors I worked with as a young director. Evening after evening, I begged her to tell me the rules of verse that Poel had drummed into her. They were substantially the same as George Rylands had taught me. But then the Marlowe Society had been founded on Poel's beliefs by Justin Brook (a distant cousin of Rupert Brooke who was also a founder member) and his contemporaries.

These traditions are precious. Does the Marlowe Society uphold them now? No. Yet they are the life-blood not only of Shakespearean theatre, but of scholarship. To study Shakespeare without regard for his form is like studying a score when you have never heard a note of music.

❖

We must start with the text itself – a record of what was said in the theatre, but not alas of what was done. Even the text is unfortunately often corrupt and uncertain. But the Folio of 1623 brings us as close to Shakespeare's theatre as we shall ever get, because it was put together by his two fellow actors and friends, Hemmings and Condle. Perhaps if Ben Jonson had not paved the way with the pretension of his collected works in 1616 (a scholarly Folio which attracted derision from his fellow playmakers), Shakespeare's actors would not have replied with the Complete Shakespeare. Half the canon – *Macbeth* and *Antony and Cleopatra* among them – would have been lost.

While the Folio brings us close to the playhouse with its book-keeper or prompter, it also poses all kinds of problems – of spelling, of lineation, and of palpable misprints. We think we know how many printers there were; and our computers help us understand their individual tastes and prejudices. But where are Shakespeare's? Lost.

The lineation – where the end of the line is, and where a half-line meets another half-line (matters which – as I will show later – are absolutely crucial to the rhythm and thus the understanding of the scene) – is variable and is often more the product of getting the maximum number of words on the page than any respect for Shakespeare's form.

Punctuation can also be very misleading. To the Elizabethans, punctuation was almost a visual celebration of rhetorical balance. But if you speak from an Elizabethan text, you realise that a comma should hardly be felt and that a semicolon has only the strength of our modern comma. Unfortunately, modern actors, working from over-punctuated, modern texts use the punctuation as a justification to chop up the lines into little realistic gobbets. In fact, punctuation should lead us on from phrase to phrase, from sentence to sentence. The rhetoric is not slow, but fast: "trippingly on the tongue". The end of the line must be lightly marked, because mainly it summons up the energy to go on. It does not droop or stop.

The problem is compounded by generations of scholars in later editions who have corrected Shakespeare's grammar and littered it with more and more conventional punctuation.

For this reason, I always work from a specially prepared text for the actors which has sense punctuation and yet keeps as close as possible to the basic punctuation of the Folio. Faced with a comma, the modern actor tends to stop. He loves pauses because he believes it makes a text sound spontaneous and "real". It does not produce speech that trips on the tongue. Nor does it maintain the shape of the line. Nonetheless, the Folio feels like a working text with the fingerprints of actors on it. Having directed it, I am convinced that the Folio text of *King Lear* gives us Shakespeare's last thoughts on that play. I agree with the current Oxford editors: it is a text cut for performance.

Hamlet's advice to the players defines Shakespeare's taste:

> Speak the speech I pray you as I pronounced it to you, trippingly on the tongue. But if you mouth it as many of your players do, I had as lief the town-cryer had spoke my lines. Nor do not soar the air too much with your hand thus, but use all gently; for in the very torrent, tempest, and, as I may say, the whirlwind of your passion, you must acquire and beget <u>a temperance that may give it smoothness</u>.

This is a perfect expression of the creative tension between form and feeling. The feeling must of course be there; but the form must contain it. Here is the paradox: by hiding the feeling, you reveal it; by not indulging it, you express it. This is the contradiction in all great acting, the ambiguity in all great art. The feeling is a very torrent, a tempest a whirlwind; yet it begets a temperance that gives it smoothness. What does "smoothness" mean in this context? Balance? Restraint? Control? An avoidance of extreme dynamics? Or sudden jagged interruptions?

Once more I invoke the crying child who moves me because he is trying <u>not</u> to cry. He is not <u>indulging</u> his emotion. And the smoothness allows us to understand and sympathise with him. If it was the opposite of smoothness – rugged, rough, intemperate, tearing a passion to tatters, to very rags – then we would recoil from it as over-the-top, unnatural, or just as plain bad acting.

There is a painful paradox here. The popular cliché of the Shakespearean actor, with his loud bombast and singing tones is <u>exactly</u> what Hamlet – and we must believe, Shakespeare – objects to. Yet to be dogmatic is dangerous: "Be not too tame neither", says Hamlet immediately, with all the anxiety of a director who wants it both ways. Your own discretion must be your tutor – you must earn what is emotional by your precision and your taste. You must decide how far you can go. Because what matters finally is that you will not overstep the modesty of nature – what is fit, what is proper, what is unhysterical – and finally, in acting terms, what is sensible and therefore acceptable. Your behaviour on the stage must always be within the context of an action that is sensible. It may be very extreme – indeed we like drama that is on the edge of the unacceptable. But every actor knows that audiences are quite capable of laughing at overacting if the performer goes over that edge.

Hamlet gives us Shakespeare's style confirmed: tripping speech, witty delivery, modest, temperate, cool (to use a word in modern parlance) yet hot in its coolness, extreme in its discretion. Finally, I think "smoothness" must refer to the line of the iambic text. Its structure must be observed and its flow maintained. There must be no sudden *sforzandos* or mis-accents in the line. It must be smooth, so that it is capable of communicating the rough. The temperance makes it acceptable.

Shakespeare wrote in iambics: de-DUM. Each iambic line uses five beats. That is its norm:

De-DUM de-DUM de-DUM de-DUM de-DUM.

If you listen to English speech, you will notice that most of our phrases run for about five beats. Hence the iambic pentameter. If you listen to French, you will notice that the phrases are longer – that there are indeed normally six beats. Hence perhaps the Alexandrine.

Shakespeare inherited the iambic pentameter as something naturally English and, by emulation and imitation, he was clearly appropriating Marlowe's mighty line, lyrical and bombastic by turn. But he transformed it, made out of it something infinitely flexible and infinitely varied. Yet the form which stands in contrast to this freedom is always there:

De-DUM de-DUM de-DUM de-DUM de-DUM.

Shakespeare's early plays have regular, end-stopped lines. The caesura break in the middle of a line, where one sentence stops and another begins, is a rarity. The extra syllable, the feminine ending –

an ancient sexist term, I presume, indicating that there is an unfinished addition to the line – is also uncommon. So the form of (say) the *Henry VI* plays is often near-ritualistic. The regular verse is often incantatory. Yet Shakespeare is already using the balance of the lines and the effect of contrast – particularly that of antithesis – to express the ironies of politics and the contradictions of power.

By the time Shakespeare is in his maturity – the time of the great tragedies and even more, by the late plays – he has a freedom in verse which is perfectly miraculous. Leontes' twisted passion and paranoia is accurately expressed by his clotted, irregular rhythms and mis-accents. But these irregularities only make emotional sense and can only affect an audience, if the actor knows the underlying regularity beneath them. He must revel in the cross-rhythms, ride the irregularities and use the bumps in the smoothness for emotional purposes. He must not give up forcing the line to scan: that tension is an expression of his passion. He must strive to make the rough smooth. Playing the mature verse of Shakespeare is much like the challenge facing a great jazz player. The beat must be kept, the rhythm always sensed. But it is the tension between that regularity and the irregularity of the speech which expresses the emotional turmoil. The nearer the verse gets to collapsing, the more tortured and emotional the expression. But it must never collapse, any more than the jazz musician can ever miss the beat or be "out". The actor must risk rhythmical disintegration, but never surrender to it. What the audience receives is therefore unexpected, dangerous, and always unpredictable. The reader should be in the same state.

It is always a shock to remember that Shakespeare's verse is his leanest and quickest means of communication. His verse does not represent "poetics". It is not poetry; for him it is the equivalent of ordinary speech. Artificiality is expressed by the prose – it is always more formal, antithetical, and ornate. The prose may also express the wrong-headed colloquialisms of Bottom or Dogberry as they strive for educated speech. But it can as well express the pretentious thought-patterns of Don Armado. It is never natural speech: it is artificial. Natural speech is portrayed by the verse – economical, fleet, often using the simplest of words so that the images when they occur may by contrast burn more brightly.

If you look at any page of Shakespeare's, of whatever period, twenty-five per cent of the lines will be monosyllabic. What does that signify? Consider the iambic pentameter which begins *The Merchant of Venice*:

In sooth I know not why I am so sad.

What do we notice about that line? Monosyllables, the sibilance of three "s"s: <u>sooth</u>, <u>so</u>, <u>sad</u>. But most of all that if we try to speak it trippingly on the tongue, if we hurry it, it loses all sense and becomes incomprehensible:

InsoothIknownotwhyIamsosad.

And so we have uncovered a startling clue: monosyllables always indicate a slowing-up, a spreading. Then the line can scan:

In sooth I know not why I am so sad.

Once again, it is the actor's task to find out <u>why</u> the line is slow, what the emotions are that would produce these measured accents. But slow it always is. There is a subtext here. Antonio knows very well why he is feeling sad – both professionally and personally. And the weighty monosyllables release the subtext.

And this brings me to another crucial point. Shakespeare's form is based on the sanctity of the line. Whatever else is jettisoned, the rhythm of the line must be preserved – kept smooth. To put in pauses and breaks:

In sooth (*Big pause.*) I know not why I am so (*Pause.*) sad.

ruins the form, and so deprives the audience of the meaning. It is certainly not smooth. Antonio's frustrations – what he is hiding and the cause of his anxieties – must be expressed by due accent and emphasis. But the line must still hold its iambic purity.

Another clue. The alliterative words are the accented words, the words that need <u>pointing</u>:

In <u>sooth</u> I know not why I am <u>so sad</u>.

"Sooth", "so" and "sad" are the operative words. By accenting them, we are already creating a wonderful counterpoint with the normal iambic rhythm.

Shakespeare is fond of beginning plays with the measured tones of the monosyllabic line:

In Troy there lies the scene, from isles of Greece…

This direct, weighty simplicity is in sharp contrast to the second line:

The princes orgulous, their high blood chafed.

The simple words of the first line set off the power of "orgulous" in the second. The word is from the French – *orgeuil* – proud, strutting, a word associated with the chivalric world of Malory and here re-coined by Shakespeare. Often the form can demonstrate how a line should be interpreted. A few weeks ago I heard an Othello bellow his great line:

Keep up your bright swords for the dew will rust them.

It stopped the riot, but it was too fast and therefore incomprehensible. It was also frantic and therefore gave no impression of the strong, certain, naivety of the character. Look at the line. First of all it is monosyllabic, so it is measured. Othello's entrance – not his line – stills the crowd and the hurried, half-iambic shouts of the brawl fall silent. We are ready for a full iambic pentameter to resolve the chaos. It must be slow enough though for Othello to think the image and for the audience to appreciate his wry wit. The inversion of rhythm at the beginning of the line and the feminine ending give it a colloquial ease and provide a strong accent on "rust". The "dew" has hyperbolical powers. This is a man defusing an ugly situation and an actor economically establishing his character.

There are a multitude of half-lines in Shakespeare – where one character hands the responsibility of finishing the line to the other character:

Peace count the clock.

      The clock hath stricken three.

The demands of these half-lines are absolute. Obviously the second actor comes in on cue; that is why there are two half-lines. But the two actors together have to make one line out of them – in tempo, tonality and rhythm. The mood and motive of each character can be completely different. But the line must not be disrupted.

So where do the characters listen to the clock striking? The normal way of playing these two half-lines is:

> (*Bell.*) Peace count the clock. (*Bell. Bell. Pause.*)
>> The clock hath stricken three.

This is not only predictable, it wastes time and is not what Shakespeare wrote. It puts a pause within the line which he specifically did not intend. If he had meant it he would have written it. What is written is this: the bell interrupts the speech of Trebonius:

> There is no fear in him, let him not die
> For he will live and laugh at this hereafter.
>> (*Bell. Bell.*
>
> *Bell.*)
> Peace count the clock.
>> The clock hath stricken three.

It is a chilling moment. The hour of the assassination of Caesar comes with the dawn, and none of the conspirators want this night to hurry away. The time is getting near to murder and Cassius knows it. Shakespeare's rhythms show this fear and it is entirely unexpected. His sense of timing is never ours.

Let me deal with a well-known scene – the first scene of *Twelfth Night* – as if I was directing it. This is the initial work I would expect the actors to do with me on the text. Character, what the character wants, his action, mood and staging come later. Much later.

The Folio gives us no stage direction about music, but clearly music is playing because the Duke is asking for it to continue:

If music be the food of love play on

Music is the most important word in the line – it is indeed capitalised in the Folio, as is "Love". This shows us the antithesis and the beginning of an extraordinary mixed metaphor. Once music has been turned into the food to sustain love, with all the associations of appetite and satiation, it needs to "play on". We are immediately in a world of deep sensuality. The line scans perfectly, the only paradox is the wonderful mixed metaphor where music sustains the life of love as food, not as melody.

The second line gives us an inversion:

Give me

The even musicality of the first line is already challenged. This is a favourite device of Shakespeare's. It surprises the audience and gives new energy to the incoming line.

We should notice the sensuality of the "s"s in "excess" and "surfeiting". Surfeiting is to run the risk of making yourself sick, to over-indulge. The line has the necessary phrase break at the end of it:

Give me excess of it that surfeiting...

What? We may ask.

This brings us to another rule. Shakespeare's phrasing is built on the end of his lines. Indeed, the end of the line is usually where the main weight of meaning is to be found. So it is <u>not</u> a place to hurry on to the next line. But it is not a punctuation point either. Say rather it is a slight lift in energy, an expectation point, like lifting the pedal of the piano on a legato phrase in order to prepare for the next. It punctuates lightly, arouses expectation, and leads us to the next statement. So what will happen to us if we "surfeit"? And here comes the answer to the question:

The appetite may sicken, and so die.

Sibilance again with "sicken" and "so". The word "appetite" is now at last invoked. Hunger and sex are equated. And the word "die" brings us to a conclusion. It is the Elizabethan slang word for orgasm. It is the finish. Satiation.

The modern actor (and reader) may very well lean on the comma after "sicken". But the smoothness of the line needs to be kept. <u>Because</u> the appetite is sickening it is dying. No break is necessary; indeed, it is destructive. The antithesis between sicken and die is clearer if the line is kept intact:

The appetite may sicken and so die.

Meantime, the music continues to play: there can be a pause after "die" at the end of the line to allow the Duke Orsino to listen to it. A pause is always possible at the end of a line, but never, never in the middle of it. A pause in the middle of a line destroys the line. If a pause is wanted, Shakespeare leaves the pentameter incomplete. The silence is written as surely as it is in Pinter.

Another rule: breaths should only be taken at the end of the line – otherwise the shape of the full line is distorted. So never breathe in the middle. This question of breathing is crucial. Modern actors are used to breathing when they run out of breath. They break up the text naturally whenever their lungs need refilling. It is a personal and idiosyncratic need. This does not do for Shakespeare. Because he requires the sanctity of the line to be preserved, he asks that the actor shall always have enough breath in his lungs to shape the full line. It is often possible for the actor to take a tiny breath at the end of the line to top up the supply of air. The lungs, indeed, should be a kind of bagpipe in Shakespeare, always full of air. The text can then be sustained.

This is not in any sense a natural breathing pattern and it is not intended to be. In the early stages of rehearsal, it is important that the actor develops a pattern so that he knows on <u>which</u> end of line he needs to breathe. Sir John Gielgud always maintains that the classical actor should be able to take three lines on one breath. This, however, does <u>not</u> mean speaking three lines as if they were one and rushing from one to another. The sense phrasing must still occur at the end of each line. The pentameter is the unit of sense – and indeed the unit of communication. It is as much as an audience can take in. If they don't know where the end of the line is, they will not understand; and if the actor does not know the end of the line, he will have no control over breath, voice, emotion or intent. To a greater or lesser degree, he will be incomprehensible. To rush on to the next line, particularly when the phrases are full of metaphor which the character is supposed to invent out of the heat of his emotions, is to sell the audience short. So the line structure must always be paramount. The actor must learn the ends of the lines when he learns the words. On the other hand, the over-marking of the end of the lines (let us not use the term end-stopped, because there should be no stop) is monotonous and sends an audience to sleep. The line-ending must be light, graceful, and almost imperceptible. And it should have an energy, an upward inflection, which is always looking forward.

Having listened to the music, the Duke comments:

That strain again, it had a dying fall.

It is a clear interruption, a command to repeat – which the musicians obviously obey. A "strain" is a shape of notes, a phrase of melody. But there are rich paradoxes here because the word has many other meanings and associations. It is a strong impulse or high emotion; it is a particular tendency or disposition. As a verb, it means to force or constrain, to exceed bounds, to find difficulty. It is clearly a deliberate word of tension. The particular reason that Orsino is envious of it at this moment is that the strain has a "dying fall" – that is a downward musical cadence, sad, finishing, conclusive. This term is also complex. It means the downward stroke of the sword, the fall to low ebb tide, the end of the bout at wrestling. But the qualifying word "dying" is the significant one. Remember that to die in Elizabethan slang is the moment when the lover reaches orgasm. So the line falls away, concluding like the satisfied lover. And that which is fallen, is no longer erect.

And this is what Orsino experiences as he savours the phrase again: he listens to the music and speaks over it as it is repeated, telling his court:

Oh it came o'er my ear like the sweet sound
That breathes upon a bank of violets,
Stealing and giving odour. Enough, no more
'Tis not so sweet now as it was before.

A great deal is going on here and the text is full of signposts for the actor. The repeat of the musical phrase earns this heavily sensual tribute. It can only be expressed by the wonderful mixed metaphors of a <u>sound</u> that <u>breathes</u> on violets, that <u>takes away</u> and yet <u>gives</u> odour. It is a giving and a taking expressed in sensual contradiction worthy of John Donne. Notice also the assonance of:

Oh it came o'er my ear like the sweet sound.

The "o"s, the "r"s and the "s"s express Orsino's orgasmic state. Several editors have suggested the substitution of "south" instead of "sound", so that the metaphors shall not be so indecently mixed. But surely the riot of contradictory senses is the whole point of the passage. We all like describing our moods, and Orsino must appropriate everything sensual in an attempt to define his own sensuality. How Shakespeare suffers from his correctors!

The elision of "o'er" gives us a monosyllabic line again. And there is a strange mis-scansion because there is an accent on "the".

Oh it came o'er my ear like the sweet sound

But elide "like" and "the" colloquially and you naturally emphasise "sweet sound". Alliteration again.

Now comes another point of great significance: we meet our first caesura – the stop in the middle of a line. Even when there is a full-stop in the middle of a line, the sanctity of the whole line again has to be preserved: otherwise the shape of the verse is ruined. This usually means changing pace at the end of the previous line so that the first half of the new line can be slowed up in order to earn the time for a full-stop. We must understand here that at the very moment of his sexual satisfaction, Orsino is suddenly overcome with disappointment and rejects the whole experience. He is wilful and changeable. What is on the surface a piece of great English lyric poetry, in fact expresses the dreadful loneliness that comes to the self-indulgent after love, whether the love be real or imagined. Here it is written out:

Oh it came o'er my ear like the sweet sound
That breathes upon a bank of violets

(Orsino is now at the point of ecstasy, the tempo changes and becomes slower, heavier, even more sensual.)

Stealing and giving odour.

(Here there is a break – but not sufficient to wreck the line, only to assert a full-stop.)

Enough no more

It is the rejection. Perhaps he suddenly realises that he is only imagining, not experiencing this love-making. And now the rhyme and the change of tone shows the depth of the disappointment and frustration.

'Tis not so sweet now as it was before.

The music has produced a totally unsatisfactory experience. He is more lonely, more miserable than he was before. Music is no substitute for his lady; and finally, is an irritant rather than a medicine to his passion.

In modern plays, directors are taught to divide the dialogue up into "beats" – or paragraphs of emotional action. A different objective creates a different mood: this gives variety of tone and pace. Shakespeare writes these changes into his verse by altering the mood of the first line before the caesura. A new complete line after a full-stop also of course provides the opportunity for a new beat, but it is not mandatory.

It has taken me many minutes to deal with eight lines. It takes me long hours to analyse the text of a play with the actors before I even suggest that they should try to perform it.

This text discipline, combined with a sense of the spoken word and an understanding of the acted word, is something that is always needed as part of the reading of Shakespeare. Orsino's speech is not a generalisation celebrating love and music. It is rather a concrete demonstration of how a man can be in love with love – and in love with himself. So he fails to find any satisfaction. In eight lines, he passes from eager anticipation to misery, and that is the dramatic action of the scene. Shakespeare is never content to rely on the power of the lyrical alone. He always gives it a subtext. We can find our way to this by studying the form: only then can we understand the action. At this moment the needs of the scholar and the actor fuse into one.

❖

Will the words of Shakespeare still be current in another two hundred years? Will he, indeed be comprehensible? The inevitable shifts in our vocabulary must mean that he becomes more difficult to understand. I am glad that I have lived at a time when an actor delivering a speech of Shakespeare's with intelligence can make an audience understand collectively what they would never have understood individually on one reading. This direct communication remains one of the wonders of live theatre. "As the bow to the fiddle…" – as Bacon pointed out. And Shakespeare's theatre is public theatre – public stimulation. Much of it is indeed public narrative. It provokes, cajoles and seduces the audience into imagining. There is no soliloquy in Shakespeare where the actor addresses himself and muses privately. Every soliloquy is a public debate with the audience. Hamlet's "To be or not to be" is a challenge to the audience. Three thousand people in daylight would never have their attention held by an actor privately communing with himself. The argument, shape, and vocabulary of every soliloquy demands the direct participation of the audience.

There is another aspect of Shakespeare that time is inevitably altering: the actual <u>sound</u> of his speech. English has naturally altered since the time of Shakespeare; language must always change. It has become more clipped and constrained, less inflected and certainly peppered with more neutralised vowels: every English vowel now aspires to the even greyness of "er". In this university, nearly fifty years ago, I learnt what was thought to be Elizabethan pronunciation. I did it, let it be hastily said, so that I and a number of others could engage in a production of *Julius Caesar* directed by George Rylands and John Barton for the Marlowe Society. We performed lustily in what was then thought to be Elizabethan speech. I say "then", because just as the agreed sound of "authentic" musical instruments varies from age to age, so I suspect do the findings of experts on pronunciation.

> (*In Elizabethan*)
> Wherefore rejoice, what conquest brings he home
> What tributaries follow him to Rome,
> To grace in captive bonds his chariot wheels?
> You blocks you stones you worse than senseless things!
> Oh you hard hearts, you cruel men of Rome,
> Knew you not Pompey?

I don't think we should play Shakespeare like that; and I am not even sure that I have it right after fifty years of remembering. But I do think an appreciation of the rich vowels and the percussive consonants (the "k" was pronounced):

Doth not Brutus bootless <u>kn</u>eel?

may encourage us to express in our own way the musical potency of Shakespeare's text. I apologise for sounding thicker than Ian Paisley in my speech. The echo of Northern Irish comes from the Elizabethan colonisers: the original accent has to some extent stuck.

❖

There is always a great deal to learn by studying the original place where a play was performed. The form of a play is very much linked to the physical conditions that gave rise to it and expressed it. Shakespeare makes sense in daylight. Greek drama makes sense in masks. And if we want to understand the nuances of Chekhov, we must begin by thinking of an early electrically lit theatre of extraordinary intimacy. The lighting is even, not spotlit; it uses floats and battens. So the setting has the overall light of a nineteenth-century oil painting – not the three-dimensional strength of a modern sculpture. In this indoor experience, we overhear the action and are disturbed by it. In the outdoor day-lit experience, we are challenged by it as if it was a public meeting.

It is unfortunately little help to try to understand Shakespeare through the customs of our own modern stages. He has always been adapted to suit the place that performed him. He was candlelit at the Restoration, in modern dress in the eighteenth century, historically accurate under Charles Kean and gas-lit, and melodramatically slow under Irving. All ages have cut his plays to ribbons in order to facilitate their painted scenery or twisting revolves. Irving finished his *Hamlet* bathed in an early limelight and cradled in Horatio's arms.

Good night sweet prince
And flights of angels sing thee to thy rest
Whilst I behind remain to tell a tale
Which shall hereafter make the hearers pale.

There was no truck with Fortinbras in those days. The Elizabethan theatre was an unrepresentational space, which, like a mask, became what the actor said it was – a palace, or a prison. We may be sure the words were audible and that they could be spoken trippingly on the tongue; otherwise, how could an audience of two or three thousand be persuaded to attend to these complex texts? They attended because they were interested in the story. And though it is perhaps a little hopeful to think that some of the plays can be got through in the "two hours' traffic of the stage", (dramatists always maintain that their plays are shorter than they are, just as they always put back the cuts for publication) played at the right pace, most of them don't come in at much more than that. I have done a full length *Julius Caesar* in two hours and eleven minutes with no interval. Unfortunately, the running times of Shakespeare have increased markedly in the last twenty or thirty years as the modern habit of playing words rather than lines, emphasising adjectives or qualifications rather than the whole phrase has become more widespread. The nineteenth century butchered Shakespeare so there was time to change the scenery; for the last fifty years, we have cut Shakespeare because we don't like speaking him quickly. We either litter him with pauses to be "real", or italicise individual words in order to insist on the meaning.

But we have reformed our stages to some extent. Since Granville Barker and William Poel, we have realised the need for scene to follow scene without interruption, or scene change. Shakespeare's scenes answer each other by contrasting atmosphere and tempo. The plays never stop: they modulate into something else as a new scene begins, and that difference is part of the dramatic argument. They are, long before Hollywood, like well-cut films. The music of the court and the lovesick indulgence of Orsino (a slow and moody prelude, if ever there was one) crosscuts to the desperate reality of the storm and Viola and the Sea Captain bringing life out of the sea. No two scenes could be more beautifully contrasted. Yet, if there is the rumble and the crash of changing scenery, to say nothing of the time taken, the contrast between the two scenes will be destroyed.

All our modern Shakespearean theatres are too large – or too small. Shakespeare demands a space where you can whisper or shout. In a studio, it is impossible to give the rhetorical energy that his more public and emotional utterances demand. Yet in the conventional thousand to fifteen hundred seat modern theatre, it is impossible to whisper. You must constantly project, and by projecting lose nuance and variety.

A few years ago, the foundations of The Rose Theatre were excavated. This was a revelation to me. I had been brought up to believe that the Elizabethan stage was a thrust, pushing boldly into the groundling's standing area. To be honest, I have always been uncomfortable with this, because when I have seen the thrust applied to modern theatres such as in Stratford, Ontario, the Lincoln Center in New York, or Chichester, I have seen a platform stage where it is impossible for the majority of the audience to see the actor when he is downstage. It is rather like a diving board: memorable for the entrance: but unless you dive off it, finally anticlimactic: there is nothing left to do but walk back again. The actor has to keep in constant movement, sharing his face out to different segments of the audience. This is a necessity in all of Tyrone Guthrie's theatres – and most markedly the one at Stratford, Ontario. Guthrie was a genius at stage movement but not a great lover of the complex text. His Shakespeare was very vibrant and alive, but he cut the text and stimulated the audience with fantastic choreography. There was always a slight feeling that the old plays were being sent-up to keep our interest. Unfortunately, verbal complexity and movement are not good bed-fellows. Shakespeare in Guthrie's theatres is in danger of becoming a physical pageant rather than a stimulating text. The ideal Shakespeare stage should be capable of both: pageant and rhetoric.

The Rose revealed not a thrust stage, but a traverse stage like its Japanese cousins. Once the traverse curtain of the central discovery space was opened, it was clear that there was a deep central acting area. With the traverse drawn the main thrust of the space was from side door to side door. The representation of war by armies marching <u>across</u> the stage made sense to me for the first time. The idea that one army could enter at the right-hand door and one at the left, and that the confrontation would inevitably lead to battle was obvious. The Rose could be an intimate space one moment, and an epic space the next. It was small enough to be domestic, yet large enough for sword fights and the sweep of battles.

The sight-lines were also fascinating. Shakespeare is obsessed by theatre imagery: "All the world's a stage"…"This great stage of fools"…"After a well graced actor leaves the stage"…being "out" when words fail the actor…and, of course, making "his exits and his entrances". But there is not one image in all the plays that relates to an actor being upstage of another. In a proscenium house this is a position of natural superiority – and an obsession with most actors. "Who has the stage?", they ask. The conflict and the tension between the upstage actor and the downstage actor is inherently dramatic. It was not at The Rose though. The sight-lines are such that wherever the actor stands – even with his back to the groundlings, way down stage – two-thirds of the audience can still see him. The only bad position is what is known in naturalistic, proscenium theatre as "fifty/fifty" – where each actor is politely at the same distance from the front of the stage and neither has the upstage advantage. They are exactly level with each other. In The Rose, such a position would mean that each actor was masking the other to half the audience. It is an untenable position. And it is never referred to by Shakespeare, because I am sure it was never used. It is current in all other forms of theatre, and to "upstage" somebody is still a metaphor of bitchiness in ordinary life. It does not exist for Shakespeare.

I think we give insufficient credit to the sophistication of the Elizabethan theatre. We should certainly know from the subtleties of Shakespeare's text that he was not writing for something crude and makeshift. The doors on either side mean that the stage can represent an inside area or an outside area. The balcony can be a wall or a watchtower. By opening the arras (the curtain over the discovery space) the whole rhythm of the stage can be changed: the thrust is now up and down. There can be an inner room at a tavern or a palace; or it is an inner area from which Desdemona's bed can be rolled out. It is infinitely flexible: Cleopatra's monument can be situated in the balcony for one scene and downstairs on the stage for the last scene. Nowhere is somewhere if you need it to be. Or the stage can be nowhere at all. It can be a place of vantage from which Duncan sees the welcoming beauty of Macbeth's castle. This, like all the descriptive passages in Shakespeare, (the coming of the dawn, the arrival of a terrible storm) are of course, all of them, to be played out front. The audience imagines what the character is seeing. No scene painter nor lighting designer can do as well.

And Shakespeare's stage played in daylight. One of the problems of modern theatre is that as we can now create darkness with our intricate lighting rigs, we often find it difficult to see. Lady Macbeth walking on the stage with a candle in broad daylight tells us much more about darkness and the horrors of night than any lighting plot. Darkness can easily be created, but then we cannot easily see the fear on Lady Macbeth's face. And if we cannot see, we cannot hear and the words cease to do their metaphorical work.

I also realised at The Rose that the entrances and exits from the side doors would work completely with the rhythm of the text. Shakespeare is adept at making surprising entrances and their rhythm is always crafted into what is spoken. Sometimes there is a sudden appearance from one of the doors; sometimes there is a long preparation as the actors walk down to take possession of centre stage:

> Here come the lords of Ross and Willoughby,
> Bloody with spurring, fiery red with haste.

Above all, it is a stage that it is easy to keep <u>hot</u>. As one scene ends and the actors leave the commanding acting space, the characters of the next scene possess it. There are no pauses between scenes, because no pauses are needed – and certainly no illustrative music.

It seems that Shakespeare and his company moved indoors to the private theatre at Blackfriars with alacrity. There was more money to be made, possibly more influence to be gained. Perhaps he loved the candles and the heat. Perhaps he loved the concentration and approved of a more sophisticated, wealthy audience. We don't know. All we know is that he continued to work in the public theatre in the summer. Perhaps his ghost is puzzled that Sam Wanamaker should have wanted to rebuild The Globe in London, when Shakespeare's last creative years were spent in the privacy and focus of The Blackfriars.

But thanks to the tenacity and vision of Sam (an American who should put the English to shame), we now have a rebuilt Globe on London's South Bank, so it is possible that there can be many experiments in the future that will allow us to understand in a more immediate way the nature of Shakespeare's playhouse. I actually do not believe in historical reproductions: they seem to me arch and undependable. What was thought Elizabethan in 1900 is not what is thought Elizabethan in 2000. I am sure that by 2100, Elizabethan will be different again. I therefore wish that the Globe, though reproducing the known dimensions of Shakespeare's theatre, had been built as a flexible modern building with modern materials and the capacity to change as new research becomes available and as (inevitably) fashions change. I am not convinced by the reproduction aspect of the enterprise, any more than I am by reproduction furniture. Historical reproductions never escape their period – any more than period costumes do. An Elizabethan dress made in (say) the 1930s will always tell us the date that it was created. Safety regulations at the modern Globe mean that the aisles are quite different, the people are quite different (a third bigger). And nothing can be done about the sound of aircraft that fill the air. It is not finally authentic. It can't be.

But authenticity should not strictly be the point of the exercise. We now have an outdoor theatre that provokes an extraordinary energy because of the relationship between actor and audience. It is a place for the imagination and therefore a place for Shakespeare. The stage will also need altering in the light of experience and new findings. A study of The Rose and what we can scan of the original Globe's foundations by infra-red must make us believe that the stage pillars at Wanamaker's Globe are in the wrong place. They are also clearly in the wrong place for practical reasons. Actors built this theatre: but actors do not build a theatre where large pillars hide them completely on their first entrance.

Nonetheless, we have a successful, living theatre which can give us a glimpse of the form that sustained Shakespeare. If the techniques of verse and the techniques of staging are now rigorously studied, we may learn much, supported by a public who have completely endorsed the building and the experience. In addition, the union at the Globe of scholarship and theatre is new and very productive. It is inevitably argumentative, and controversial. But out of the arguments will come new understandings.

The energy of Shakespeare is still palpable. There are over seventy Shakespeare festivals in the United States. Shakespeare is still alive – just – on our British stages. I say just because by the time I was twenty, I had seen the entire canon on the stage, several of the plays many times. That was in 1950. It would not be possible today.

But the understanding of the form and shape of his writing seems to me in decline and that is one of the reasons why the young find it increasingly difficult to understand him. In a visual age which values spontaneity and sensation above technique, the knowledge of how to play Shakespeare's texts and how to read them may very well not survive. It is urgent that we learn to value his form again and that we learn from form rather than distrusting it. I think, in sum, that possibly for the first time in four hundred years, practical theatre has a crucial part to play with scholarship in getting us closer to Shakespeare and maintaining his potency.

MOZART'S ENSEMBLES

Mozart's Ensembles

A uthenticity is a will-o'-the-wisp. It is unfortunately not an absolute: it changes from decade to decade. Is the Mozart of Glyndebourne in the Thirties, with the recitatives recorded on a piano, more misleading to our ears than today's astringent, authentic orchestras, beating the timpani with hard sticks and using no vibrato for the strings? Authenticity is an attempt on the part of each age to bring itself closer to the original creation. Sometimes paradoxically it is content to reinterpret the past: I am sure the nineteenth century thought that their vast choirs were flattering the composers' intentions, bestowing on Bach and Handel a power they would have loved to have had. Authenticity changes with each age as the evidence is argued over and re-evaluated. It should not surprise us that it varies so wildly.

Fashions keep changing, and whatever we learn by study or creative deduction, we must always remember the obvious fact that "authenticity" can never be achieved because we can never have an authentic audience. On the other hand, the correct scale of performance has an enormous effect on the experience. Hearing a string quartet in a small room makes us understand the true meaning of Chamber music.

So although I am probably deluding myself – as all animators of the classics are prone to do – I believe we are closer today to Mozart's style than we are to Shakespeare's. In a sense, this is inevitable: Mozart is only two hundred years away from us. But both geniuses have been seriously warped by time, and by the way we perform them. Yet it cannot be denied that in the last twenty years, reducing the musical forces, playing in appropriate spaces and in period styles, has all had the effect, I am sure, of making us understand the nature of Mozart better. This has not quite happened yet to Shakespeare.

It is difficult for us now to understand how casually Mozart was regarded, even seventy years ago. He has never not been popular, but he tended to be minimised as the decorator, the charming, tinkling boy of the eighteenth century. We now have a better appreciation of his heart, mainly because we appreciate his ambiguities. *Così fan tutte* is no longer cold and immoral, but an unblinking look at the fickleness of the normal human heart. Mozart is the new individual challenging the blandness of the Enlightenment, the near-romantic confronting the classical tradition and yet remaining a classicist.

Artistically as well as politically, Mozart was writing at a watershed of history. The eighteenth century knew very well what music was and should be. Mozart's energy questions this certainty: his sudden shifts of key, his chromaticisms, the challenge that so many of his phrases offer to the forms of the eighteenth century, not only point the way to Beethoven and the Romantics; they enable him to express heartbreak and pain in counterpoint to the order of the classical world. He deepens music. In his hands, it takes on a tragic dimension.

❖

We start again with the text. The modern obsession in music is to find the purest, the earliest Ur-text: a composer's first thoughts are usually deemed his best. And original instruments – or at least original methods of playing – are studied so that Mozart may be cleaned, as an ancient painting is cleaned. Everything is done in the name of authenticity (which is certainly not true of Shakespeare). Most surprisingly, cuts are not made, they are restored.

In the theatre, it is alas quite different. Music critics would protest if a few bars of Mozart or Wagner were ripped out here and there in order to speed things up and satisfy our short modern attention span. But chunks of Shakespeare are removed from the plays without most of our drama critics apparently even noticing. Or if they notice, they remain indifferent either to the sins of adaptation or omission. A recent production of *Hamlet* cut the great first scene. This interested many. Some found it quite original that in substitution the audience watched a home movie of old father Hamlet gambolling on the lawn with his young son. A lot of these contortions are attempts to stimulate the jaded palettes of people who have perhaps seen the plays too many times. And it is certainly a way a director gets noticed. But in sum, we have to admit that we moderns are quite as daft as Nahum Tate with his happy ending to *King Lear*, Charles Kean with his panoramic view of Athens at the time of Pericles which started *A Midsummer Night's Dream*, or Beerbohm Tree's real live rabbits in the midsummer wood.

Having had some experience of how rightly protective Samuel Beckett and Harold Pinter are of their texts, I wonder what Shakespeare would say if he saw the delicate rhythms of *Twelfth Night* disrupted by a director who decided to put the second scene first. I have seen it done. Some even thought it more logical. It arguably is: beginning with a storm – as Shakespeare later demonstrated – gets things off to a tumultuous start – and allows the play to begin with a universal symbol. But in *Twelfth Night*, it makes for obvious melodrama and it isn't Shakespeare. We must start with Illyria – must be drawn into that heavily self-indulgent world – before reality, in the person of Viola, arrives from the sea.

In the theatre, directors often cut something because they say it does not work. It is more often because they do not know how to make it work. To cut the text because it has lost all meaning and is truly incomprehensible seems to me regrettable, but permissible. But in fact there is – as yet – quite little completely dead text in the canon. If the actor understands, the modern audience still understands. To cut and edit in order to give Shakespeare a new interpretative slant seems to me hubris of the worst kind. It is something we would never do to a composer.

Music is obviously the primary language of opera. It sets the mood and the tempo; the timing of the actions and the heat of the drama. It can support the words so that they are clearly audible as narrative. It can illustrate them, or it can play against them. It can contradict them. It is all pervasive. The first section of a *da capo* aria can take us as far as a speech in a play; an eloquent musical phrase as far – and sometimes further – as a line of blank verse. Music is a mask for drama. And it is like a good mask in another respect – it can mean anything. A phrase of music begins as something completely neutral. It can be sad or happy, dramatic or pathetic.

It can frighten or reassure, put us to sleep or urge us to dance. The choices are infinite and it entirely depends on the treatment of the phrase by the composer – the tempo, the harmony, the dynamics.

Listen to Beethoven's *Diabelli Variations* and you will realise the truth of this. Beethoven takes an ordinary little theme, that had been circulated to a group of composers by the publisher Diabelli, hoping that each would contribute an original variation. Beethoven at first declined, then changed his mind and defiantly made a huge master-work out of this most unpromising material. He teased and pounded it into the most surprising shapes, and out of banality, he makes a disturbing pilgrimage from the naïve to the spiritual. A jingle becomes a symphony.

Mozart has a similar breadth. His mastery of the orchestra ensures that he is always an alert dramatist. The action and the atmosphere are created by the orchestra. And this is subtle and surprising – but never blatantly illustrative. If the singers listen to the orchestra as they act, and follow the orchestration, they will understand the shifts in the psychology of their characters. Horns bray and mock as Figaro contemplates cuckoldry; woodwinds chatter away in irony to highlight the Count's pomposity; and warm clarinets show the sensuality of Susanna. The orchestra acts for the characters. And providing the singer maintains a state of relaxation and neither over-illustrates the music nor contradicts it by his actions, the drama will happen almost inevitably.

By the time Wagner finished *The Ring*, this beautiful, naïve directness had been complicated. Mozart's characters must fill their hearts with what they hear as they perform, and behave accordingly. But Wagner's characters can be only occasionally aware of the complex tapestry of leitmotifs which surround them. It is Wagner, not them, who is speaking to the audience through the orchestra. He sets himself up as the all-seeing Homeric bard – perhaps even as the Maker himself, drawing cross-references and parallels, ironies and coincidences in a godlike way as the drama unfolds. He looks forward and he looks back: he is above the characters, like a figure of destiny reminding the audience what has been and what will be, as leitmotif contrasts with leitmotif. Wagner's orchestra is therefore a cosmic chorus, underlining the dramatic ironies. Occasionally the leitmotif comes out of the character; sometimes it directly illustrates the character; but mostly it is a reminder by the composer of how to interpret his drama and understand the tangled skein of fate. This is knowledge that the characters only apprehend fitfully: the audience are reminded of it all the time.

But Mozart is Shakespearean in his music – an easy term, but I promise you responsibly used. Mozart's sense of form is absolute, yet he is, like Shakespeare, completely free in it. His masterpieces are also quite as ambiguous as Shakespeare's. Indeed the three operas he wrote with Da Ponte – *Così fan tutte, Le Nozze di Figaro, Don Giovanni* – are fables which revel in contradictions and arguably fulfil the brief of all great art: it asks the right questions yet does not patronise us by returning simple answers. Leave that to propaganda art.

Da Ponte's witty and perpetually scatological verses are set against the elegance and proportion of Mozart's music. They produce a tension which is consistently dramatic. Yet Mozart's experiments with tonality make him able to plunge suddenly into the depths of pain. This dangerous contradiction is what makes him seem so very modern to us. The nineteenth century often thought him inconsistent – even flippant.

Mozart's theatre was tiny and of course indoors. He wrote for auditoriums holding only at the most four or five hundred people. Since his death, opera houses have steadily grown bigger, orchestras have played louder, and the dramatic pretensions of opera have become more grandiose, pompous and generalised. Singers fortunately have remained the same size. But it is an unequal struggle. They are no longer the fresh voiced youngsters of Mozart's day, because they must produce a volume that can ride over the sonorities of a modern orchestra. Neither are they witty and text-based, as the original singers must have been. The true image of a modern opera production is a superstar in a bright follow-spot trying to sing down a virtuoso orchestra. And all this is in huge auditoriums before three or four thousand people. Even the precise orchestration of Mozart can be coarsened in our new large buildings. He wrote for the human scale – an auditorium small enough for the performer's eyes to be seen, their thoughts to be recognised, and their inflections understood. Communicating irony is necessarily a very subtle thing. But this is Mozart's language and he demands this subtlety; the delicate interplay of one character with another then works – eyes meeting eyes, emotions affecting emotions.

In our time, the old Glyndebourne and Drottningholm in Sweden were the only two major opera houses intimate enough to <u>act</u> Mozart.

Now Glyndebourne has been replaced by the magnificent new house with its splendid acoustics. But the eyeball to eyeball intimacy of performer and public has gone. We need a new Mozart house to do for him what the new Globe may yet do for Shakespeare.

Opera is action conveyed by the mask of music. But it needs the right performance space and very demanding conditions. It requires a long, close collaboration between singers, conductor and director through meticulous, shared rehearsal. And what binds all these disciplines together is music – the form. The actions of the characters in the drama of course affect the nature of the music-making. And then the music-making critically affects the drama. Which comes first? Neither. Opera has to be a perfect circle: the drama making the music and the music making the drama. Only by analysing the interplay between text, music and action and expressing them through mutual creative decisions between conductor and director is there any hope of achieving this difficult synthesis. We may have good music; we may have good drama. But to fuse the two is a hard task. A director gives up half his kingdom when he works in opera. The conductor, not him, is in charge of timing, atmosphere, pace – and finally emotion. So the conductor must know why the dramatic decisions have been taken because he has to translate them directly into music-making. On the other hand, a conductor can too readily find a director who places the singer so far up-stage that the balance of the voices is ruined, or one who does not recognise that a tricky musical entry demands that the singer must see the conductor. Director and conductor have to be equal (which they are usually not. In most opera houses, the director takes second place because his craft is less defined, less demonstrably technical than the conductor's). But for the work to live, they have to collaborate closely and leave their egos outside the rehearsal room. On the rare occasions when this happens, opera makes perhaps the richest form of drama.

Mozart can no more be over-emotionalised than Shakespeare can be cried or ranted. Once more we must strive for "a temperance that will give it smoothness". Discretion, form, yes, smoothness allows the containment of violent emotion. This is as true of the *legato* line of Mozart as of the iambic pentameter of Shakespeare. Yet both can express complete emotional dislocation by slightly disrupting that form. But the balance of the musical phrase and the regularity of the iambic pentameter remain the mask which makes expression possible. By hiding, we reveal; by containing, we concentrate.

Mozart's solo arias work in exactly the same way as Shakespearean soliloquies. The mask of public behaviour, which enables a character to react to the other characters, is taken off and the audience is allowed see the truth – his truth, naked and uncomplicated. Emotionally, the aria is the heart of the matter. Don Ottavio's *"Dalla sua pace"* in Act One of *Don Giovanni* was added, I am convinced, not only to please an ambitious tenor for the Vienna premiere, but also to give the audience an early and essential understanding of the true character of the man. Up to this point, Don Ottavio has been strong, understanding, helpful in the face of dreadful crisis – in a way, a surrogate father to the betrayed and neurotic Donna Anna. We may indeed suspect that he is nearly of the same generation as his friend the Commendatore, the father of Donna Anna, who is tragically killed by Giovanni in the first startling scene of the opera. We move from *dramma giacoso* to high tragedy and back again with the speed of lightning. It is deliberately unsettling.

In this crisis, we may believe that Don Ottavio is an entirely suitable match for the great man's daughter – steady, firm and calm. The aria, always providing that the emotions are shared completely with the audience, reveals the inner man. It is a surprise. He is not so careful, not so meticulous after all. He has a wild, passionate tenderness, and an active love for this wayward girl. He becomes, therefore, the positive representation of love in the opera – the strong moral force, well able to match up to the evil indifference of Giovanni. The Don flaunts his sins in order to challenge God: he wants Him to prove His existence. He boasts to the heavens of his sexual conquest to see if there is anyone there. Don Ottavio by contrast is steady and purposeful, the very embodiment of the strength of goodness. But this aria proves that he has passion in his virtue. He is not a weak romantic.

If Don Ottavio sings this aria to himself, he risks making us feel that he is repeating something that he already knows. The effect may be romantic in a broad sort of way. It will certainly be "operatic" – which means generalised, emotional – and what is expected in opera. But the aria has a specific action: it is the revelation of his strength; and we should feel amazed at seeing his mask removed. We should now like him and sympathise with him – and that is why the opera needs the aria. Its true drama is betrayed (just as the full drama of the soliloquy is betrayed) if it is not given public utterance – as narration to us, the audience. The reader of the score must therefore always remember that these arias are public debates. The audience response is as necessary as it is to Hamlet's soliloquies. And for that, you need a small theatre.

The need for public demonstration of what the secret heart is feeling, is even greater when we come to the Ensembles – those unique glories of Mozart's operas. He is always the great innovator, taking existing conventions and revolutionising them. *Singspiel* becomes heroic and spiritual as well as popular comedy; *Opera Seria* is no longer artificial but humanised with deep feeling; *Opera Buffa* (as in the three great Da Ponte operas) becomes startlingly modern, psychologically subtle, rather than obviously comic.

For Mozart, the Ensembles are a new and rich means of dramatic expression. An extremely artificial form (when three or four voices join to sing in a mini chorus, usually in agreement) becomes in his hands something contradictory and dramatic. It reveals the human comedy in the most complicated way. Unfortunately, the conventions of naturalism have profoundly damaged our understanding of Mozart's ensembles and our ability to perform them. Most opera houses now get them musically right but dramatically completely wrong.

Ensembles – a trio, a quartet, a quintet, even a sextet, depend for their drama on the direct address of the audience by the characters. The text that they all sing is the same, but the individual meanings are different, because their motives and their moods are different. Musically, a proper ensemble demands a fine sense of balance: the music must blend. No singer must out-sing another. But he must, if the drama is to work, actively try to out-act the others. He must behave as if he and he alone is talking to the audience. The disparate attitudes of the characters – sometimes even their blatant contradictions – produce the drama and the comedy. We hear what they are all thinking inside themselves at this moment of frozen time as they put their case to us, confident of our support. And we see that they completely disagree. Their thoughts and emotions are in sharp contrast; but musically these disparities are set in the smoothest imaginable music.

Singers in Mozart Ensembles usually either stand rooted to the spot, carefully blending together as if the drama were over and the concert had begun; or they desperately bend the text so that they sing the same words to each other in happy agreement. This takes away all tension, and all dramatic meaning. Mozart's main use of this marvellous device occurs in Act Two of *Figaro*. The finale is constructed with a series of ensembles – trio, quartet, quintet, sextet, septet in a symphony of increasing intrigue, misunderstanding and pain.

In Act Four of *Figaro* he uses the device to express even more complications. Cherubino flirts in the darkness of the garden with the figure that he believes to be Susanna, the maid. Actually, it is the Countess who has disguised herself as Susanna in an attempt to catch her own husband making love to her maid. Unknown to them, they are observed by Figaro, Susanna and the Count. These three are unaware of the presence of each other. At this point of rich complexity, the Countess, Susanna, Figaro and the Count all sing the same text to the audience, believing, each one of them, that they are the only person speaking and that the audience implicitly agrees and endorses everything that they are saying:

Se il ribaldo encor sta saldo,
La faccenda quastera

(If the scoundrel stays any longer,
He'll ruin everything)

The four characters have very different emotional states. The Count is full of jealousy for Cherubino, because he sees his assignation with Susanna disappearing. Figaro expresses blacker jealousy: he sees his plot to catch his wife with the Count about to be wrecked by Cherubino – whose attentions to his wife are, incidentally, not repulsed as strongly as he would like. The Countess is distraught because she sees her plot about to be ruined by the recklessly flirtatious Cherubino. Discovery is imminent and Susanna, not for the first time on this mad day, sees with her usual unblinking clarity, that the ice is in danger of breaking. All their lives are about to be wrecked.

These enormous complications are expressed all at once in a short section of the ensemble. The crisis is conveyed to the audience in a daring economical way. Mozart is using a device which is unique to opera. If four people speak at once in a play the result is incoherence, even if they are saying the same words. Even if their speech is drilled with the utmost precision the effect is abstract and inhuman. And to be comprehensible, they have to speak in time: that is, speak in unison. With this complete uniformity, no difference of attitude will be audible. But in opera, and particularly in Mozart's operas, we can look at each one of the four characters for a split second and then move on to the next, comparing their different attitudes as they sing different phrases. Our eyes cut between them, like a shrewdly operated camera. Each voice must be audible, yet they all make a musical whole. We listen to the same text from each of them, but we take in the ironies because in every mouth the text means something different. The same words reveal the painful comedy of different people caught in the same crisis. Only opera can deal coherently with the emotions and words of several people at once. Only opera can exploit the paradox that we all have different responses to the same situation, even when we are saying the same words. And for us – the audience – it is a moment of complete chaos made clear. The music gives it form and meaning.

In a sense, each character is playing the scene alone with the audience – or should think that he or she is. And unless the singer understands the competitive nature of ensemble acting (which is the complete opposite of ensemble singing) – the need to talk to the audience as directly as a soliloquising hero or heroine, or a stand-up comic – and unless all of this is done in a small scale theatre, we are left, not with tense, living drama but with a purely musical climax.

❖

The particular form of drama developed by the nineteenth century was naturalism. It was their revolutionary form, their reality – their mask. For the first time, rooms were presented with four detailed walls – though one was removed so that the audience could see in. Before this revolution, doors and windows had been painted on the backcloths; entrances were made through the wings. But now the doors were real, with catches and locks and latches. Windows had curtains. Bookcases had books. This theatre of reassuring realism tried also to make time into a reality. Forty minutes on the stage was forty minutes in life – or near enough. All this was as authentic as could be. Shakespeare's impressionistic tricks with time, when he passes through a whole night in a ten minute scene or speeds up the action so that what was expected tomorrow happens today, and then suddenly ends up as now, was thought unrealistic and therefore incredible. Acting tried to simulate natural behaviour and dialogue pretended to be real speech, modestly inflected and spoken at a near-natural volume. So theatres had to get smaller. The German *Kammerspiele* became the ideal. Actors no longer told the audience their emotions; they suppressed them under a text which purported to be everyday conversation which the audience overheard. Drama as narrative declined. Drama as a jigsaw of apparently realistic pieces that the audience had to collect and assemble in order to understand the back-story and then proceed to watch the crisis (the plan of most of Ibsen's prose dramas) became the fashion. This theatre reached its climax with Ibsen and Chekhov. And they – like all geniuses – tried to break the mould at the very same moment that they accepted it. They pushed naturalism to such poetic extremes that it became almost as metaphorical as the classical theatre that preceded them.

Although their audiences were privileged voyeurs, peeping in on a simulation of ordinary life, Ibsen and Chekhov are both formal writers whose dialogue goes far beyond ordinary speech. Chekhov's subtext – what we experience under what is said – is his heart. The surface is deceptively ordinary. Ibsen's constantly reiterated word patterns (there is a particular vocabulary for each play, a cluster of obsessional words) reveal the inner frantic natures of his locked-in characters. The Norwegian language has a very small vocabulary. Repetition is therefore forced on Ibsen's characters. Ibsen translators who revel in the rich quantity of synonyms in English and vary the words do the characters scant justice.

In Chekhov, understatement, and in Ibsen, obsessive repetition make a tension between the seeming naturalism of the action, and the particularity of the speech. From the middle of the nineteenth century, lesser talents imitated ordinary speech, even the speech of the street, and wrote naturalistically without shape, economy or a particular style. Lesser talents still do: it can be heard every night on television.

The naturalistic revolution of the nineteenth century was of course as embarrassing to the conventions of opera as it was to the conventions of Shakespeare. Much like the classical theatre, opera was based from its beginnings on the conventions of public storytelling and public performance. The audience was part of the action. In Monteverdi or Cavalli or even in the *Opera Seria* of the eighteenth century, a solo aria is always, like a soliloquy, a direct emotional address to the audience.

The singer opens his heart to the spectators and, indeed, always tells them the truth. (He only dissimulates or tells lies to the other characters in the drama.) The singer must of course feel his emotions deeply, but he also tells them to the audience at exactly the same instant as he feels them. And so he involves the audience in his predicament.

This performance of narrative – of a character telling rather than indulging his emotions – has an ancient history which takes us all the way back to Homer and to tribal storytelling. And it is of course at the centre of Shakespeare's drama – direct address being the readiest way for him to hold an audience's attention and tell his story.

But by the second half of the nineteenth century, opera conventions were becoming uncertain in their use of classical form. The great finales of Verdi – supreme in their music – often seem uneasy in their drama. Characters and chorus join in a huge summation of musical and verbal themes. Who are the characters singing to? Themselves? Each other? They are only fitfully involved with the audience: there are none of the contradictions or direct debates that Mozart's characters enjoy. And in the great chorus scene in *Götterdammerung* (whose libretto admittedly belongs to an earlier convention) the address is neither public nor private when Wagner comes to add the music. The fourth wall of naturalism is an uneasy barrier: the vassals are not clear whether they are an abstract Chorus of performers singing in an opera, or characters acting in a drama. Wagner was obviously happy to lose the ancient audience contact. The Bayreuth opera house, with its invisible orchestra, gives the composer a chance to speak directly to the audience with his music. Beyond the invisible orchestra, there is a mythical stage. The audience is encouraged to look at it as if they are watching a distant dream. The public storytelling and debate of Mozart and Shakespeare is no more. Opera is now a place of misty illusion. And the orchestra tells us what to conclude in the foreground.

In contrast, Mozart's theatre was always frankly a theatre: stage and auditorium were equally illuminated with many lighted candles. There was almost as much light on the audience as on the performers. So the communication between them must have been complete – certainly better than we have in our days of electricity and huge darkened auditoriums. And Mozart's drama depends on a performer's ability to see his audience and speak directly to them. In a large modern opera house, the singer can barely see his audience, and in any event has difficulty making contact over the wide orchestra pit. To remove the social mask in order to talk to a black empty space feels irrelevant, if not foolish.

Mozart's theatre is very much about the mask. This preoccupation with illusion and reality, with social deception and emotional truth is expressed through the constant obsession that Da Ponte and Mozart have with impersonations. Leporello disguises himself as Don Giovanni and is credible enough to seduce the hapless Elvira. The Countess disguises herself as Susanna, and is credible enough to deceive her own husband. Guglielmo and Ferrando in *Così fan tutte* disguise themselves as officers from another country in order to find out which girl loves them. By disguising themselves, they find themselves. They should therefore be "realer" – more normal – disguised than not disguised. Then it is clear why the women fall in love with them. This reversal can be very eloquent if the performers look more like their natural selves when they are disguised.

Disguise is at the heart of Mozart's drama. It must be treated very seriously and done very well. This is not the facetious device of the old comedy, but another of Mozart's brilliant reformations of the conventions. He constantly makes comedy into something serious; and then the serious unexpectedly becomes funny. But it must all be based on reality. Leporello therefore has to be the same size and shape as Don Giovanni, otherwise the love scenes with Elvira simply become comic improbabilities and make a fool of her. Even worse, if the scene is played for comedy, the anguish expressed by Elvira provokes laughter as Leporello serenades her. The laughter should of course be there, but mixed with very real pain. Chekhov loved Mozart.

For the same reason, Susanna and the Countess must credibly change persons. All the people in these operas who are deceived, must be well deceived. Otherwise we are betraying Mozart's serious intentions.

There is some evidence that Mozart's original singers enjoyed the vocal challenge of disguising their singing so that they sounded like the people they were imitating. It seems to have been a theatrical effect well liked by their audience and presumably well done by the performer. It should be disturbing as well as amusing – as any perceptive imitation will be. It is at heart, satirical. If we think of the maid imitating the Countess – and doing it well – we can perhaps understand why *Figaro* was thought a revolutionary tract before it was loved as a heart-stopping opera. Nowadays, the vocal imitations are hardly even attempted. We are just not good enough at them. And they are very difficult.

If a Count can become a servant, and a servant can become a Count, rank itself is in question. All this role playing – this changing of class and status – is of course revolutionary. Mozart and Da Ponte were out to show that man with his clothes off, man in the bedroom, is much the same animal whether he be aristocrat or peasant.

A man's clothes do not make the man – it is his heart that matters. As they wrote, the French Revolution was just over the horizon.

I have said that Mozart's audience was illuminated as much as the singers. Just as for Shakespeare, audience and actors existed in one space. This can help us understand the drama. In a candlelit theatre, when Figaro walks on stage and announces that it is very, very dark, the audience accept the fact, even though he is very well lit. From then on, they will imagine that it is dark. As Figaro acts that he cannot see a thing, the audience continue to see him very clearly. They can therefore also understand and appreciate all the mistaken identities of Act Four because, unlike the characters who are pretending that they are in the dark, the audience easily recognises everybody. By the light of that even candle-power, they can understand what the characters are feeling. In the literal naturalism of our electrically-lit theatres, we are expected to make darkness, because, at the press of a button, we can make darkness, just as we can make light. If Figaro tells us it is dark in a modern opera house, we expect it to be dark. Otherwise the action is not credible because the gap between what we see and what we are told is too great. So the performance is conducted in darkness. But in this naturalistic gloom, it is impossible to follow the plot or the emotions because we cannot see who is who. And if we are allowed to see them, we don't believe that the characters cannot see and recognise each other. What was an essential theatrical strength, because the audience imagined darkness and yet could still see, has become literal and unconvincing.

Darkness is a central obsession of Da Ponte's. Night is a time for mistaken identities, for sensualities; a time for reversals, indeed for revolutions. Act Four of *Figaro* is impossible unless we believe in the velvet darkness of that very sensual night.

There is much else that we can learn from the beginnings of these masterpieces. We know that in Mozart's day, pitch was a semitone lower, so the high notes were produced with less tension in the singer's throat. We also know that the orchestral sound must have been generally quieter – because eighteenth-century instruments had nothing like the attack or sonority of their modern counterparts. But they were clearly the right accompaniment for Mozart's generation of singers. Nancy Storace, the original Susanna, was seventeen when she created the role. The first Don Giovanni was just twenty-three. No one would be allowed to sing these roles at those ages today; the strain would be thought to endanger the future of the voice. We must therefore try to imagine what Mozart was dealing with: young, fresh voices supported by a delicate texture of orchestral sound. Da Ponte complains about many things, but he never complains that his words cannot be heard. For a man of his verbal precision and wit, words must have been very important. They still are; but we hear less and less of them.

Nonetheless, I suspect that Mozart would have been delighted by the virtuosity and size of our modern orchestras – just as he was delighted by the Mannheim Orchestra when he encountered it on his travels. It is clear that the technical standards of instrumental playing have improved beyond recognition in the last two hundred years. But I wonder whether Mozart – and Da Ponte also – would have liked the large voices that we now need to ride over this volume of sound? Would they also have liked the fashion among many modern singers to suppress their consonants and become virtually incomprehensible in order to preserve the shape and beauty of the vocal line? I doubt it. This is carrying smoothness too far. I also doubt therefore whether communication has improved generally. The music is so predominant in much modern opera singing that it is sometimes difficult to understand what language is being sung, let alone what it means. Delicacy, precision, real *piano*, real *pianissimo* and a relish for the words, so that their ambiguities and paradoxes may be enjoyed, must have been the necessary objectives for Mozart. The music must have been more subservient to the words and the drama. Such a balance and such clarity are not easy to achieve today.

A few years ago, Simon Rattle gave some revelatory performances of Mozart operas with the Orchestra of The Age of the Enlightenment. The music was naturally quieter because of the period instruments and period playing techniques. The consequence was that Rattle could unleash the drama in the orchestra with little fear of drowning the singers. Because he did not have to hold the orchestra back, the orchestra, although quieter, was much more vivid than its modern counterpart. It could be a wholehearted contributor to the drama.

Mozart's three operas with Da Ponte are all about the pain of love – and specifically about the misery occasioned by sexual attraction. The hurt and the frustration are in the music. The erotic atmosphere is there too – but it is also in the words. Only the English Restoration dramatists – Wycherley, Congreve and Dryden – can rival Da Ponte's love of double entendre. I sometimes think that these sly obscenities were slipped in to entertain Mozart, to make him giggle as he composed; it is difficult sometimes to find any other purpose. Are the characters aware of the implications of what they are saying or not? Are we dealing with the unconscious blunders of Dogberry, or the deliberate double-meanings of Horner in *The Country Wife*? Generally, I think the characters are aware. Mozart's characters are not mealy-mouthed. There is no nineteenth-century prudishness – rather an appreciation of the absurdity as well as the pain of sex, its ridiculousness as well as its pleasure. We are dealing with wit and usually salacious wit.

There is another problem for opera performances today and particularly for the text-based Mozart: the blandness of much classical music-making. We live in the CD age, and to be a constant seller, the compact disc performance aspires to be middle-of-the-road and never eccentric. Accuracy in music is of course essential, but a market which avoids the personal or the unusual interpretation (because constant replayings make the oddities irritating) is in danger of not personalising music at all. Many opera recordings are, in the interests of being glossily unexceptional, basically undramatic. The first recordings of the great singers of the golden age in the early part of the twentieth century reveal a procession of talents that do not hesitate to bend the music to their own personalities. It is exciting stuff, but it would never be allowed today. It is too personal.

I love the classical music heritage and have spent a great deal of my life working in opera. But I must confess that the music that always compels me is great jazz, because there is a tension between the form and the freedom of the player which is truly dramatic. Jazz musicians mean what they play. They must: they create it. Too many classical musicians simply play what somebody else means, what is written down. They are expert, but they are bland. They leave it to somebody else (usually the conductor) to provide the meaning. But a jazz musician must mean something emotional in his own right – otherwise he cannot play. He is truly a soloist and must embrace the form of the music, and then improvise as a personal response. A great Shakespearean actor – Olivier at his best, Scofield at his best, Ashcroft at her best – is like a great jazz musician. The shape of the verse is meticulously preserved and the rhythm of the line is always respected. But, like Sidney Bechet, the articulation is always nearly off the beat. It is that instant of nearly being off, which makes the audience feel that it is natural, free. It makes the formal into the natural and enables it to express natural feeling. It no longer sounds like conventional Shakespeare or Mozart when a master performs it. The speech, the singing, the jazz become unique – made for this moment, unrepeatable. It can never be played quite like that again. The artificiality of the mask – whether it be verbal, rhythmic, or musical – once more achieves a simulation of human reality. The mask is the recognition of form, but it must be nearly destroyed to live, not slavishly followed. Too much music-making today is proud of its ability to repeat itself accurately.

Great operatic acting is largely a matter of complete relaxation and stillness so that the orchestra can do the work for the singer. When this is achieved, the performer's whole body becomes a mask for the music. This is difficult because the act of singing forces the windpipe into a monstrous state of tension in order to produce the note. With that centre of energy so pressurised, it is difficult to get the rest of the body to relax. This is why singers, and particularly tenors (the most constricted of them all), are often awkward on the stage. Large gestures in a state of high tension only make matters worse.

All in all I think that Callas is the greatest operatic performer I have ever seen. The clichés about her are always that she was "tiger-like" and "paced the stage". Strictly, this is not true. She was an extremely still performer, and yet very relaxed. That was her mask. She appropriated, it seemed, the entire orchestra so that its drama appeared to be coming directly out of her. Seventy-five men and women in the pit playing for her? No. All the energy and all the drama of the music seemed to be coming quite simply, out of her. The slightest movement released tumultuous music. But it was all entirely without tension. It was relaxed because she gave herself completely to the form of what she was performing.

The anxious opera singer illustrates emotions by making movements that respond to the music or executes huge gestures in a vain attempt to match a musical climax. This never works. In the right state of relaxation, an entire orchestra can be working for the singer. "Filling-in" – as it is called among opera singers – where the singer provides some physical movement or gesture as he finishes singing in order to do something while the orchestra reaches a climax, simply destroys what has been built up.

In any form of drama, we experience emotion, we understand character in action, not by wild improvisation or by intemperate feeling, but by the form. The singer learns his notes, and then works on the musical phrase to see what he needs to feel to make the music a true expression of his feelings. It is the same for the actor. Learn the words first, understand the form first and then see what you need to feel. This is the opposite of what modern drama schools teach. Generally they consider the formal demands of the text after they have analysed the character and what he is feeling and what he wants. The assault on form has been with us for a century as a consequence of the psychological theories of Stanislavsky and by their offshoot, the American Method – a system which brilliantly helped people to act by improvising text or by approximating to the text. It is no accident that it was developed by American actors for many of whom English was the second language. It was strictly non-verbal, about pauses rather than speeches, sobs and hesitations rather than complex metaphors. It was a technique that was emotion-based, and not form-based. And yet it produced some memorable results. Play the video of Kazan's great film of *A Streetcar Named Desire* and follow with the text. Brando gives a performance which is wildly inaccurate to Tennessee Williams' lines, and which almost entirely ignores his punctuation and his phrasing. Does it matter? Not to Brando, nor to us when we see Brando. Once more genius makes its own rules. But if you are not Brando, the way into Williams' drama has to be his form – those long, complex sentences. Not the Method.

Great dramatic writing is very near to music. It is as organised, as precise and as economical. And music is always inherently dramatic – particularly when it appropriates words and succeeds in making us think at the same time as we feel. In both theatre and opera, it is the mask that we need to study.

All substances clothe themselves in forms; but there are suitable true forms and then there are untrue, unsuitable. As the briefest definition, one might say, Forms which GROW round a substance if we rightly understand that, will correspond to the real Nature and purport of it, will be true, good; forms which are consciously put round a substance, bad. I invite you to reflect on this, it distinguishes true from false in

Ceremonial Form, earnest solemnity from empty pageant, in all human things.

Thus Thomas Carlyle – an unlikely philosopher to hammer out a thought that we can use to define the nature of good theatre and the nature of bad theatre. Because the integrity of form <u>does</u> distinguish good art from bad art; honest creation from calculated attitudinising.

But art must always challenge, always disturb, always provoke. And this applies particularly to the performance arts, which are public and therefore social. So in the theatre and the opera, though we must accept form, we also have to challenge it so that it almost breaks down. It must never be allowed to deaden us. It must express our emotions not inhibit us. This tension makes the young classical draughtsman into an iconoclastic Picasso; and the jazz musician becomes unique because he personalises the phrase – and nearly misses the beat. Out of the tension between form and freedom comes emotion. But original dramatic creation, if it deals with the writer, must always start with his form. It is the beginning not the end; a discipline which may seem to bind the performer but will end up in freeing him. To understand this is to understand Mozart and to understand Shakespeare.

THE METAPHORS OF
BECKETT AND PINTER

The Metaphors of Beckett and Pinter

D rama can be expressed in many ways – mime and song, dance and shadow-play, mask and marionette. But whatever the means of representing dramatic action, nothing for me surpasses the power of the word, and particularly the power of the word when it defines or prompts that action. In plays, the word defines silence. In opera, the word inspires the composer to create the music. Allied to the word, the half-anticipated, yet still surprising change of key recharges the action. Shakespeare's words can provide us with great antithetical paradoxes that illuminate the mind; and his metaphors fire the imagination in scene after scene.

In the theatre, the word always focuses. It is the telling of the story, the narrative that holds an audience. And it is the word that makes theatre complex and ambiguous. Pinter's eloquent and emotionally shattering pauses are created by the words that surround them. He speaks by not speaking. The paradox of the life-enhancing despair of Beckett is conveyed by the beauty of his Anglo-Irish cadences; and the long, lyrical sentences of Tennessee Williams (with their great dependent clauses from the deep South, always redefining, qualifying, expanding) reveal the heat of his characters' emotions at the very moment that they are trying to hide it.

I have found that the most useful guide to directing a living playwright's work is to listen carefully to his speech. Not his dramatic speech, but his speech in life. The tone of his voice is naturally never far away from his dialogue. Whether it be Pinter's assertive, staccato phrases that are followed by sudden silences; Shaffer's infinitely antithetical qualifications; Stoppard's dry yet highly illuminating wit; David Hare's cryptic and passionate dialectic challenges; or the rueful, haunting repetitions of Samuel Beckett, they all help us hear the writer. It is invaluable knowledge for the rehearsal room.

These modern masters are often thought to write naturalistic dialogue. But of course they don't – just as Ibsen and Strindberg didn't. All of them are in a sense <u>poetic</u> dramatists. They use words – even colloquialisms – as metaphors that mean much more than their literal sense. All good dramatists have a style that is personal to them – a precise style expressed by an individual voice. But however formed their dialogue may be, it can never be allowed to destroy the audience's belief that they are sensible to accept it as normal speech. If it lacks that conviction, they will judge it artificial. It may well be on the borderline of acceptance: that is the excitement of much of Shakespeare's craggier verse. But however structured and formal it is, the audience must always finally accept it as "real" speech.

Just as in the classics, the phrases of the principal modern dramatists are formed and crafted. They have a shape and an economy and a precision which the actor ignores at his peril. If he tries to make Pinter more "naturalistic" by ignoring his pauses, or Tennessee Williams more colloquial by splitting his long sentences into Brando-like stutters, he will simply ruin the potency of the writing. And it is not easy to play any of these dramatists. Their form must be assimilated and endorsed like an intricate piece of music. Bernard Shaw's sentences need pursuing to their very ends if the energy of his arguments is to be kept dramatic. It is a disaster to play him slowly or to play semicolons as full-stops. I never met Shaw, but I have heard recordings of him. He is always the public orator, hypnotising us with the torrent of his words. And that is the basis of his style and the style of most of his leading characters. Shaw is the Fabian idealist who has the energy to make political rhetoric sexy. Play him naturalistically, and you dry out his characters and they cease to be people.

❖

How does the use of language differ between plays and novels, or between plays and poetry? The novel can be naturally discursive; the pace can be slow or speedy. There is time. There is also always a productive tension between the authorial voice and the dialogue spoken by the characters. Something may be said; but the author can tell us what is really meant.

Poetry to be read can obviously be much more complicated than speech designed for the stage. There is a limit to what we can untangle in the theatre in the fleeting moment. An audience never has much time. And on stage, the actors know it takes only a few seconds to lose the audience's attention for minutes, if not for good. A line that is unclear or pretentious (or badly spoken) can drop the tension and lose the audience's belief. So our playwrights must give us language that is packed, arresting, multi-faceted, and set it in a dramatic situation which supports it or may indeed sometimes contradict it. There is frequently tension between what the line says and the context in which it is delivered. This makes drama. Oberon's:

I know a bank where the wild thyme blows,

begins one of the finest lyrics in the English language. But it is delivered by a character who is enjoying the beauty of the flower-decked wood because it is in malicious contrast to his purpose. He aims to drug his wife so that she falls instantly in love with a passing monster, horrible if possible:

Wake when some vile thing is near

is how this rhapsody ends.

In this fairy world, love leads inevitably to lust. After the heady description of the flowers, the bathos of this line should get a laugh. And any dramatist will tell you that if an audience laughs, they have understood. The plot is now set up for the arrival of Bottom the ass.

The language of a play is always informed by the dramatic situation. And this tension must be cultivated and understood by the reader. He or she must never forget that this is public utterance, designed for a public space. It is not possible to go back, to read it again or to hear it again. The communication must therefore be instantaneous. It may be that the words are being used to cover rather than parade the emotions of the characters. The reader must also understand that when this is enacted live, the hiding paradoxically reveals the emotion. Chekhov's characters are constantly exposed by their masks. Or the words may be straightforward, plain up-front narrations of emotional states as in Greek drama or early Shakespeare. The reader is dealing then with the palpable, not the hidden or the qualified. In soliloquy, the character will be dealing with direct public address, so the reader must never forget the response from the audience. A live audience has high adrenalin: it has a quick instinctive apprehension of words, a love of wit, a love of surprise and a love of metaphor. And it is very ready to laugh. An audience is quicker than any reader, more instinctive, and collectively more intelligent than most of the individuals who make up its numbers.

Perhaps naturalism in the theatre is therefore not enough – it can be seen as a limited, and often inadequate use of the theatre's imaginative power. We can now see the last one hundred and fifty years of naturalism as a passing phase. The theatre can do more, much more than convince the audience that they are watching a slice of real life. And though masters like Strindberg, O'Casey and Williams transcended naturalism with their dialogue and made great efforts to strip away the unnecessary realities of their stages, most theatre was until recently imprisoned in a literal representational style that became increasingly moribund. It was inert because it had lost its metaphorical strength, its capacity to mean beyond itself. Opening the curtains in Ibsen was a strongly illuminating symbol for the audience of 1870 because until then the theatre hadn't had window curtains to open. It was therefore a metaphor that had an impact. Light was being let in on darkness and the characters were likewise confronting reality.

But today, the action is unremarkable and ordinary. At most, it is decorative. And if we understand its metaphorical meaning, we will judge it as obvious. Its potency has not taken long to fade.

T. S. Eliot wrote:

> A verse play is not a play done into verse, but a different kind of play...The poet with ambitions of the theatre, must discover the laws, both of another kind of verse and of another kind of drama.

I would go further. I believe that no play is worth our attention <u>unless</u> we can describe it as a poetic play. Because only the poetic play makes metaphors rich enough to persuade the audience to play the essential dramatic game of make-believe and use its imagination.

But I do not mean necessarily a play that uses poetry in the literary sense; rather a play that uses all the vocabulary of the theatre – word, action, visual image, subtext – to be dramatically poetic. In our age of the screen, provoking our imagination is the unique strength of the theatre – the imaginings encouraged by a live performance. Poetic theatre can deal with the widest subjects, the most improbable transitions. We can imagine we are anywhere. We can imagine the heights and the depths of feeling. Though verse is not a prerequisite of this metaphorical potency, form is – it represents the means to encourage a metaphorical interpretation of the play's language or action. Or both. Too often for Eliot and his contemporaries (Auden, Isherwood, certainly Fry) the term "verse play" indicates that verse has been tacked on to a prosaic text, the images decorating it like a collection of sequins on a rather homespun dress.

The desire to return to poetic drama was obviously a reaction to the naturalistic revolution, but I think it misunderstood how imagination is provoked in the theatre. The so-called poetic revival of the late 1890s with the plays of Arthur Symons, Yeats and Stephen Phillips were responses to the naturalism of Pinero, Shaw, Galsworthy and even of Granville Barker.

But the great plays have always been and always will be poetic plays. Granville Barker is to me a poetic dramatist because though he created a verbal style as particular as Henry James, it is acceptable as the speech of men. Shakespeare did it so consummately that the British wonder every forty or fifty years why others don't follow him. So there is a "poetic" revival – usually with fanciful language grafted on to workaday dramatics. But the revival is inevitably self- conscious. Antonin Artaud called for a poetry of the theatre, rather than poetry in the theatre. I subscribe to that. Artaud has given a precise description which will serve for any great drama. And it will serve for Shakespeare's verse: he writes poetry of the theatre, not poetry in the theatre.

> The aim of the theatre as a whole is to restore its art, and it should commence by banishing from the theatre this idea of impersonation, this idea of reproducing nature; for, while impersonation is in the theatre, the theatre can never become free.

So wrote Gordon Craig at the beginning of the twentieth century in *The Art of the Theatre*. (This is still an essential book for anyone who believes in theatre.) What Craig proclaimed has now actually happened. The theatre is freer of decoration, freer of unnecessary reality than it has been for one hundred and fifty years. Less is clearly more. Yet it is one of the few experiences left in the information age where we need other people. It is a <u>social</u> place – a place of communal imagining. The stage is art – but it is an art where the concrete emotions of the particular word provoke the imagination to understand the ambiguous and the intangible – even to understand the at first incomprehensible. It makes a rich game of make-believe. Paradoxically, the game grows stronger and stronger as film dominates more and more of our lives. The camera records reality, and what it photographs in imaginative terms is inert. A picture on the screen is not perceived as other than it is. It may represent fantasy, but it is not fantasy; and its achievement is no spur to the imagination. We are not asked to imagine that the screen image is something other than it is. The camera shows us what it wishes us to see. Indeed, it imagines for us.

If I walk on to an empty stage and launch into a speech telling you that this is Rome, you believe me if I am a good enough actor and my text is sufficiently stimulating. If a camera is brought in and I am filmed telling you that this is Rome, you then look at the projected film and say, "It is not Rome at all, it is an empty stage." You cannot play a game of make-believe on the screen. The camera does not transcend the visual images that it shows. What is there, is what is. A play of Shakespeare's therefore cannot breathe and have its being on a screen even in the most remarkable Shakespearean film. Shakespeare is generally not about evocative images but evocative words. The language therefore distracts from the images of the film. Film does not need language that provokes our imagination; it needs images that we can see and react to. My preferred Shakespeare films are therefore all in foreign languages – Smoktunovsky's *Hamlet*, the Japanese *Throne of Blood, Ran*. None of them are embarrassed by the imaginative demands of Shakespeare's text. Of all the Shakespeare plays I have seen on the screen – in cinemas and on television – and all the opera videos I have seen, only a very, very small percentage actually seem "true" and therefore capable of fulfilling George Burns' demand for honesty. Let us restate it, adapted: "The thing about theatre is to create the truth. If you can fake that, you have got it made." Most poetic theatre doesn't fake on the screen, because it cannot fake. Indeed, it simply looks fake – as if an old-fashioned piece of theatre or an old-fashioned production of opera had been recorded by the camera and shown up as the artificial thing that it is. The camera has no imagination. The camera is itself the form – not what it photographs. So leave Shakespeare in the theatre where he needs words and imagination; and leave opera in the opera house where we can imagine that singing is speaking. Videos and films of either of them are good adverts – good bits of PR for the real thing. But they are like reproductions of famous paintings: they may well win converts, but they are far from being the thing itself.

❖

I must now try to define more closely what that poetry in the theatre is. In this last lecture therefore, I will briefly consider how two men have brought metaphor back to the modern theatre: Samuel Beckett and Harold Pinter. Neither of them are "verse" dramatists. But both of them deal with a highly wrought form of dialogue which is personal and metaphorical. And both of them have filled their stages with metaphors that go far beyond naturalism.

Beckett led the way in the 1950s. His language is selective and particular. His use of the stage has created images that haunt the modern imagination. Two tramps stand by a road, waiting for something to happen, for someone to arrive; a woman is buried in the earth: in the first Act, she is up to her waist; in the second, up to her neck. These are images that represent the process of living. Then three heads in a row of urns; a spot-lit mouth…The images are reduced to what is completely necessary for the meaning of the play. There is no decoration. And by this economy, Beckett regains a total philosophy of the theatre, where the words and actions fuse.

Without Beckett, the way would not have been made straight for Pinter, for Bond, for Mamet or for Kushner. They have all continued to challenge naturalism; they all work to give the stage back to our imaginations. I am going to analyse two beginnings – *Waiting for Godot*, and *The Homecoming*. I have chosen beginnings because in both cases, the stage is still and the slate is clean. We must look at the beginning of each play as if we know nothing. It is, after all, in the first five minutes of any play that you feel glad that you have come or decide glumly that you shouldn't have bothered. It is the time when the scene is set, the theme announced; the time when the audience senses, however instinctively, where the play is going – and, in narrative terms, what it is going to be <u>about</u>. It is the time therefore when in these examples, the metaphor is announced. Let me analyse these beginnings as if they were evidence that I was sharing with the actors for the first time.

First the text. It should go without saying that the text should be the most accurate and considered available. In our non-verbal world, actors and even stage-managers are often content with approximations of what the dramatist wrote. In the average television play, it does not matter much. Indeed, the actor's colloquial adaptation is often better than what was written. But in Shakespeare, or even Denis Potter, it does matter. And in Beckett it certainly matters. If the actors are to be absolutely accurate in punctuation as well as word, then the text must be incontrovertible.

Godot is a particularly thorny problem for the scholar, the student and the actor. It exists in many texts, because Beckett went on adjusting and amending the dialogue through a lifetime of productions. The only completely accurate text, which enshrines Beckett's final thoughts on the play, is found in Volume One of *The Theatrical Notebooks of Samuel Beckett*, published by Faber & Faber, unfortunately at seventy-five pounds. All the other available texts are superseded or untrustworthy. It is sad to think that this masterpiece of the twentieth century continues to be disseminated round the world in corrupt texts. But then, so does much of

Shakespeare...The text is of absolutely primary importance because this is the beginning of the discipline, the beginning of the mask.

Beckett calls his play a tragi-comedy. This is a surprisingly forthright statement from a usually equivocal author. Act One begins with very spare stage directions:

(*A country road. A tree. A stone. Evening.*)

We are in a world of minimal expressionism, where less is very definitely more. In fact, at this moment in the 1950s, modernism entered the theatre. Up until the mid-century, the theatre was liable to decorate itself and to use its stages – which in those days were predominantly picture-frame stages – as pictures. A "country road" is a temptation to any designer. But proliferating trees or abundant bushes will undermine the pure statement that Beckett wants to make. I know, because that is what I mistakenly came near to doing in 1955 when I did the first English language production of the play. The author wants "a tree". One tree. We shall understand this precision more when we see what it is there for. It is a tree of hope in springtime, but also an untrustworthy means by which a man may hang himself. It is a means of life, and an inadequate means of death. The tree, and the stone, are the only constants. The day comes and goes, the night comes and goes, the moon rises and sets, but the tree and the stone remain. You can rest on the one, or hang yourself from the other. They are the environment. One changes, the other is still. The tree changes in the second act: it sprouts leaves.

Spring has come. Life goes on – just. There are only four or five leaves.

There is a rewrite contained in these stage directions. Beckett added "a stone" at a very late stage of his life. With it, the environment is complete. Vladimir stands by the tree; and Estragon sits on the stone. We are on a country road with two unexplained, undescribed characters; Vladimir stands upright, half in shadow, listening. Estragon is seated, still, head bowed. There is a long silence. And then the spell is broken.

Beckett describes the first actions. His stage directions are extremely precise and reflect the importance of mime in his plays. Mime too is part of his text, part of the given, part of the metaphor, part of the form. The intricate routines that Winnie in *Happy Days* executes with the contents of her handbag – the toothbrush, the powder compact, the mirror, the lipstick – are a physical description of how she passes the time and how she combats growing older. They are an absolute ballet. And at the heart of Beckett's elaborate descriptions, there is a concrete meaning.

Compared with Pinter, or with modern dramatists in general, Beckett is lavish with his stage directions. But they are not psychologically descriptive, like the anxious directions of Eugene O'Neill. He lards his dialogue with melodramatic descriptions, perhaps because he fears that what his characters speak it is not quite as emotionally charged as he would like it to be. His dialogue is indeed "impersonation" – to use Craig's term and at its colloquial worst, it has little form. Hence it is pumped up so that the actor is instructed to speak it "with savage eagerness"; or "worried and pleased at the same time". Or the stage direction attempts to make the moment more important:

> *(Draws himself up with a stern pride and dignity and surrenders himself like a commander against hopeless odds.)*

It is faintly ridiculous. Actors loathe such descriptions. It is doing their job for them, and doing it badly. It describes an end result and doesn't tell the actor emotionally how to get there. But with Beckett we have simple actions, not melodramatic descriptions:

> *(Estragon tries to take off his left boot. He pulls at it with both hands, grunting. He gives up exhausted, rests, tries again. As before.)*

There is a rhythmic precision in all this. Then:

ESTRAGON: *(Giving up again.)* Nothing to be done.

The instinctive voice of despair, from the man sitting on the stone. The Celtic soul perhaps. Certainly there is something in the rhythm of the line that makes one think of O'Casey and of Synge. A strong double emphasis in the line:

Nothing to be done.

Who are these men? We don't know. They are on a country road and already we understand that they are waiting. What for? Immediately we are plunged into the central action of the play. It is as relevant and as economical as that other great beginning:

Who's there?
Nay, answer me. Stand and unfold yourself.

When I first read *Godot* in 1955, I thought that
these characters were tramps. It wasn't a conscious
decision. It never occurred to me that they were
anything else. They were men in big, worn, smelly
boots, sweat-stained bowler hats and baggy trousers.
But there is no description of what they are or what
they aren't. Over the years in different productions
they have been many things – clowns, convicts,
intellectuals, peasants, young men, old men, women.
They are all of us of course. And they have endured
most human experiences. Their back history can be
deduced from the text, and it is very comprehensive:
war and peace; art and religion; music and
disputation. Survival. Many later productions –
including Beckett's own – enshrined the tramp idea:
they were vagabonds, men living rough who had
known better days. So we are plunged into an
immediate rich, metaphor of the theatre. The men
are waiting. It is a metaphor for life.

ESTRAGON: (*Giving up again.*) Nothing to be done.

VLADIMIR: (*Advances, halts.*) I am beginning to
come round to that opinion. All my life I have
tried to put it from me, saying Vladimir, be
reasonable, you haven't yet tried everything.
And I resumed the struggle. (*He broods, musing on
the struggle. Turning to ESTRAGON.*) So there you
are again.

Vladimir, the intellectual, the equivocator, the
philosopher. He is part lawyer, part Jesuit priest. He
is neurotic and questing, ironic and ever hopeful.

We quickly understand that these two are like a
man and his wife, arguing their way through life:

VLADIMIR: So there you are again.

ESTRAGON: Am I?

VLADIMIR: I'm glad to see you back. I thought
   you were gone forever.

His sarcasm is reproachful. This is immediately recognisable and accessible. It is the deflation of the cross-talk comedians – of Morcambe and Wise, of Abbott and Costello. The tradition of vaudeville. It is also the deep instinctive rhythms of claim and counterclaim which are audible in the voices of any two people who have lived together for many, many years.

VLADIMIR: Get up till I embrace you.

ESTRAGON: (*Irritably, rejecting him with both
   hands.*) Not now, not now.

VLADIMIR: (*Hurt, coldly.*) May one enquire where
   his highness spent the night?

ESTRAGON: In a ditch.

VLADIMIR: (*Admiringly.*) A ditch? Where?

ESTRAGON: (*Without gesture.*) Over there.

VLADIMIR: And they didn't beat you?

ESTRAGON: Beat me, certainly they beat me.

VLADIMIR: The same lot as usual?

ESTRAGON: The same? I don't know.

Their irritation with each other betrays their love; their constant bickering, their complete dependence. There are no holds barred.

Notice the particularly Irish cadences. Notice the beat of the prose. It has a rhythm and a quantity, a rhetorical certainty, born of public speaking and of words not as instruments of a subtext to hide our feelings, but as the means by which an emotion or an idea is expressed or argued. Catholic disputation. Beckett had the ability to write this play in French, in German, and in English. He did texts in all three languages. Yet even in another language, it is the voice and literary traditions of Ireland that we can hear.

In the Seventies, Beckett did a beautiful production of *Godot* himself at the Schiller Theatre in Berlin. He wrote out the entire production, move by move, gesture by gesture with many little diagrams. And it is this prompt book which is printed in the edition I spoke of earlier. It took him many months to execute, and the method of working – to tell the actor precisely where his left hand should make a gesture, where exactly he should move his foot - is not, to put it mildly, in the tradition of creative directing. We are taught instead to encourage emotions that will lead an actor to move, and that such a suggestion will make the move more spontaneous than telling the actor to move as a decision already made by the director.

When I asked Beckett why he had written what was in effect a drily factual record of the staging of a *Godot* production, he answered: "Because I am not a director. I am a writer and I have to write it all down or else it doesn't exist".

So he dictated to the actors the moves he had imagined and written down. The actors initially found this a dreadful imposition because they were constrained into a series of physical patterns. They then, somehow, had to make the moves their own. It took them, they told me, many months. By the time they had done so, what was on the stage was a production of genius. But it arrived there by a dangerously dogmatic means. Genius makes its own rules.

As the play proceeds and we meet the paranoid, anxiety-ridden Pozzo and his slave, Lucky, we move into the harsh world of power politics and human dependency. The talk between the two tramps remains poetic, though it is always laced with the feed and pay-off of the music hall. It is rhythmically precise, and depends on the rare gift of the great actor – timing; add to a sense of timing, a clear technique. There is a famous exchange later in the play:

VLADIMIR: That passed the time.

ESTRAGON: It would have passed anyway.

The feed is "passed" and "time". The pay-off is "anyway". But the laugh will only come if the feed is correctly inflected and rhythmically precise. Feeds are always more important than pay-offs, which is why in a double-act, the comedian is entirely dependent on the talents of his straight man. These two, however, change roles constantly: sometimes Vladimir is the straight man, sometimes Estragon.

Godot has a beautiful musical form, and many haunting silences which define speech. And speech itself is our way of defining, questioning, understanding and entertaining each other as we wait. It passes the time, to talk, to quarrel, to dispute; even though it would have passed anyway…Lucky, the servant with the fused brain, still has the urge and the instinct to define and question. But in his great speech, his thought processes are dislocated. They have their own logic, but they do not achieve coherence. The connections are all tangled up. There is a total loss of coherence, but tragically no loss of memory.

Beckett is lyrical, yet harsh. Precise, yet sensual. He, more than any other writer of the twentieth century has brought poetry back to the theatre as something organic. The ancient devices of the rhetorician – paradox, balance, antithesis – are there in abundance, just as they are in Shakespeare. Yet Beckett's speech has no pretension. It can always pass for the speech of ordinary men. It remains sensible. Even Lucky's tirade – a mass of words delivered from the tumult of an over-charged brain – is energised by the desperate attempts to define by finding the right word. But the right word sets fire to many others, like a match landing in a box of fireworks.

Beckett's stage is a metaphor. And the actions that Vladimir and Estragon go through – the waiting, the disappointments, the realisation each day that Godot once more has not come, is a potent image of our incomprehensible life. Yet because it has shape and humour, form and economy the overall effect is positive, not negative. At times, these two have compassion for each other – even love. So man endures. Man has hope. Perhaps Godot will come tomorrow.

❖

MAX: What have you done with the scissors?

(*Pause.*)

I said I'm looking for the scissors. What have you done with them?

(*Pause.*)

Did you hear me? I want to cut something out of the paper.

LENNY: I am reading the paper.

MAX: Not that paper. I haven't even read that paper. I'm talking about last Sunday's paper. I was just having a look at it in the kitchen.

(*Pause.*)

Do you hear what I'm saying? I'm talking to you! Where's the scissors?

LENNY: (*Looking up, quietly.*) Why don't you shut up, you daft prat?

(*MAX lifts his stick and points it at him.*)

The opening scene of Harold Pinter's *The Homecoming*. The influence of Beckett is immediately evident: the rhetorical devices of the repeated word "paper", "paper", "paper"; the insistent tensions in the rhythms. But there is something else here that has clearly developed <u>out</u> of Beckett: the use of silence as a thing of dangerous eloquence.

The unsaid becomes almost more terrifying than the said. Pinter actually <u>writes</u> silence; and he appropriates it as a part of his dialogue. Woe betide the actor who has not decided what is going on in the silence. It is as eloquent as speech and must be truthfully filled with intention.

The stage is as much a metaphor in *The Homecoming* as in *Godot* with its road, its tree and its stone. Here we are in a room. Practically all Pinter occurs in a room – a defined, protected place of uneasy security – uneasy, because it may be invaded at any moment. But this room has already been opened up. There has already been a violation:

(*An old house in North London.*

A large room, extending the width of the stage.

The back wall, which contained the door, has been removed. A square arch shape remains. Beyond it, the hall. In the hall, a staircase, ascending U.L., well in view.)

We learn later that the room has been opened up, "to make an open living area". There are no secrets in this place. Everything is "well in view". It is a public area where this all-male family fights out its battles between the father and his sons, in full view of everyone. There is no door to shut, so the metaphor of the set is potent from the very beginning: it is a dangerous space. And the hostility between the characters is evident from all the threatening pauses – from what is <u>not</u> said. We will discover the back-story, the curse on the family, as the play proceeds. It is almost as potent and terrible as that which dogs the house of Atreus in another very different kind of family play.

The basis of Beckett's drama is the precise rhetoric and equivocal irony of the Anglo-Irish philosopher priest. The basis of Pinter is the cockney "piss-take", much beloved of London taxi drivers. To take the piss out of someone is to mock them, to make them insecure. But the successful piss-taker must not let those from whom he is taking the piss know that he is taking it. His mockery should rather be masked by charm and concern. The hostility is deeply hidden, the malice completely covered. Lenny consistently makes his father uneasy by staring pleasantly at him. Or by simply ignoring him. He insults him with charm and care. This is a master taker of piss.

Underneath all of Pinter's dialogues, there is always a seething melodrama, strong hates, forbidden lusts. Underneath the mask of the speeches there are high passions which the actors must know and yet almost never reveal. To show your feelings in Pinter's world puts you at a fundamental disadvantage. You are weakened once your motives are known.

Very occasionally, of course, feelings come to the surface. They either become too hot to hide, or they are goaded into revelation. Then sudden violence erupts. A man's head is cracked open; a catatonic fit seizes the victim. Violence may run very deep, but it is always present.

I rehearse Pinter in much the same way as I rehearse a Greek play in masks, or a Shakespeare play in verse. First there must be a rigorous study of the form. The repeated patterns of speech, create rhythms where the precise accenting of words is crucial. And then there are Pinter's trademarks: his Pauses. They often put form into nearly colloquial speech. There are three types: Three Dots in Pinter is a sign of a pressure point – a search for a word, a momentary incoherence. A Pause is a longer halt in the action where the lack of speech is a form of speech itself. A Pause is a threat, a moment of non- verbal tension. A Silence is longer still. It is an extreme crisis point. Often the characters emerge from a Silence with their attitudes completely changed. We should feel what happens in a Pause; but we can be frequently surprised by the state of a character as he emerges from a Silence. The change in him is unexpected.

These three signs are all areas of turbulence – the Three Dots, the Pause and the Silence.The feelings must be hidden, hidden inside the actor, nonetheless. But all the pauses have to be filled by the actor (and understood by the reader). They are moments of very great emotion. And although the characters are hiding what they are feeling, they must feel it nonetheless. It is easy to read Pinter quickly, jumping over his various pauses as if they were unimportant. The reader, as well as the actor, must decide what is going on.

It is also easy to denigrate Pinter's pauses. He once rang me up and announced a re-write: "Page thirty-seven", he said (I found page thirty-seven). "Cut the pause". There was a twinkle in his voice as he spoke, but he was dead serious. The placing of the pauses and their psychological importance has been meticulously considered by the author. One of the miracles of live theatre is that an audience can always sense what an actor is feeling without the actor having to <u>show</u> that feeling. So the feeling must be there, though hidden. Playing an enigma is impossible. It is therefore necessary as part of the rehearsal process to go through Pinter's scenes exposing the hidden violent emotions as if the actors were playing in a melodrama. They expose their motives completely and show their hatreds and their loves in extreme terms. The next task is to hide these strong emotions again – contain them, bottle them up. But now the actors know what they are hiding. If this process is not followed, I find that the Pauses and Silences can become empty and make the dialogue sound abstract and pretentious. But the pauses must be <u>earned</u>. Unless the audience can follow the hidden emotions through the Pause, they often do not understand the journey that the characters are making. The vacillations can seem unmotivated, even ridiculous. There is a danger then that the audience will laugh <u>at</u> the play rather than with it. This can easily make Pinter seem an Absurdist, someone as joyfully surrealistic as Ionesco. But Pinter is too fundamental and true in his emotions ever to be an Absurdist. So is Beckett.

For me, there are therefore three stages of work on a Pinter play: a study of the text, where the form and the rhythm are understood; the Silences and the Pauses and the Dots are learnt precisely, and the repetitions of antithetical phrases are considered. This is a formal, technical work process. Accuracy is essential.

The next rehearsal must cautiously use the methods of Stanislavsky. The psychological processes of the characters and what they want have to be understood. I say "cautiously" because this cannot result in improvisation or alteration of the dialogue or the pauses. If the actor feels uncomfortable with the text once he has found his motive, then the motive is wrong, not the text. A conductor would be surprised if one of his first violins rose from his desk and said "I can't play this A Flat: I don't feel like it." But many actors believe themselves justified in questioning a line if they feel that their character wouldn't say it. Very occasionally, this can be a valid objection. But the danger of course is that however true the actor's instinct may be, what he wants to represent may be more conventional, less original than what the author envisaged. So the actor has to realise that when he is dealing with a real dramatist, it is usually the character that the actor has created that is wrong, not the line.

The third rehearsal process is playing the melodrama which lies underneath the text. The hottest of passions are unleashed before they too are masked. In Pinter, the mask is at the same time the enigmatic tool of communication and the main way in which human beings protect themselves from each other.

Pinter is to me the most poetic of the post-war crop of English playwrights. His form is complex and intensely studied. And it is his form which makes his dialogue crackle with theatricality. He can be a very lyrical writer, as a play such as *Landscape* reminds us. But above all, his form allows him to explore the terrifying hostilities between his characters. They fight duels not with swords, but with words and silences. Beckett and Pinter have restated that the theatre's strength is metaphor, and that its potency is primarily invested in language. They have shown the way, but is it the way to the future?

What kind of drama and what kind of stage shall we have during the next century? Will the theatre survive? Is it dying? Its imminent death in the West has been prophesised regularly over the last five hundred years, either by hopeful puritans or indifferent governments. I think at this moment it has, blessedly, a uniqueness which could ensure its future.

What will it be? A theatre led by imagination and freed of literalism? Or a computer driven populist miracle of lasers and acrobats and virtual realities? This might assuage the guilt of our new Roundheads, our New Labour government who seem to regard anything challenging in education, broadcasting or the arts as elitist. All of these cultural disciplines, by their very nature (and particularly the arts) are liable to be "off message". I believe we must strive to keep them so.

The theatre now has modern responses. It has moved decisively out of the picture frame in the last hundred years. The visual rhythms of Appia and Gordon Craig and the shapes revealed by the use of brilliant spotlights on textured three-dimensional objects have turned the magic lantern pictures of the gas-lit Victorian theatre into the stark sculptures of modern design. As less has undoubtedly become more, the imaginative possibilities for the audience have also increased. While the picture frame has been progressively discarded, the stage itself has projected further and further forward until it has created again the intimacy of the Regency theatre or the epic intimacy of the Elizabethan stage. We have all wanted to make the performer and the audience inhabit <u>one</u> space, not two. The interaction of audience on performer and performer on audience has thus become stronger. Everywhere theatre people have striven for the same thing – an intimate, yet epic space. A Shakespearean space. I believe this movement will continue.

Old theatres, like the pre-1997 Royal Court or the RSC's Aldwych or Peter Brook's antique ruin at Buffes de Nord in Paris are all spaces where the actor and the audience become one. Old auditoriums are easier to play: they are usually impure geometrically, avoiding straight lines and full of curves. They are also full of ghosts and dirt. We should treasure them. One of the difficulties that the twentieth-century theatre has had to surmount is that modern architects tend to deal in pure geometry. An audience, left to its own devices, naturally sits on the floor in a half-circle, confronting the performers. They make an impure space, not a piece of modern architecture. They do not sit in straight lines.

Practically every major theatre built in the last fifty years is too big. A society that judges success mainly by the strength of the market must demand more and more seats. Unfortunately, actors cannot be made larger – only audiences. To register and understand the unspoken means that an auditorium cannot hold more than about seven hundred people. This is theatre. It is uneconomic certainly, but it is equally certainly deprived of its subtlety if it is much bigger. Charge a price that reflects the actual cost for these seven hundred seats and you will have an elitist audience of the rich and inevitably in time an unprogressive aesthetic which clings to the past and consequently produces dead theatre. A good audience is never made up of one class – poor or rich, young or old. It must be mixed, as our society is mixed. But these mixed groups who gather in the theatre are still an elite in one respect: they are all eager for theatre. Good theatre gives society better television, better film and ultimately, through the joy of play, more educated children and more cultured adults. So just as we pay for health and pay for education, we should pay gladly for the performing arts. For me, the social case for subsidising the arts remains incontrovertible.

It would surely be a paradise to live in a democracy mature enough to pay its artists to criticise it. In art, he who pays the piper should never call the tune. It destroys the point of learning from our artists if we tell them what they are to say to us. Unfortunately then, the problems of the theatre's future are political rather than aesthetic. Do the electorate care about it? The politicians think not.

❖

I believe that we need live theatre more than ever. We need it above all to challenge dogma and to ask difficult questions in an increasingly simplistic and commercialised society. Our culture is over-influenced by advertising, unexceptional global television and journalism made sensational so that it may the better entertain and gain bigger audiences. Sadly, like our educational system, it if we do not cherish it and pay for it, the theatre will not flourish. Also, like our educational system, it cannot be judged only on financial grounds. For a democracy, theatre is all-important for another reason: it is one of the few occasions left when a segment of society can engage in a live debate with itself.

As a nation, we are apathetic about these needs. We are very good at creating theatre, but perfectly awful about cherishing it. Politicians can't and don't care about long term issues – I suppose partially because these issues do not catch the headlines of today. And politicians certainly don't care about the arts. They suspect there are no votes in the arts and while they think it, they will be right, because they endorse a philistine rather than a creative culture. Encouraging children to enjoy a rich life of play and providing the art for them when they are adults that they have learnt to appreciate as children <u>are</u> long-term issues. Even if politicians care individually about the arts, they don't collectively. My experience of both parties is that they are wonderful to the arts when they are in opposition. Yet I believe that the theatre will become increasingly important in future years and that society must be persuaded to look after it. Academia and the theatrical profession both have a responsibility for this.

In this new information age, we shall live and shop and travel and learn – and even to some extent entertain ourselves – by means of information technology. All those vast hypermarkets that have been built on both sides of the Atlantic may soon become the empty palaces of the past. We shall not longer shop for the basic repetitive purchases of life, like cornflakes or soapsuds; they will be bulk-bought on the internet and delivered to our homes. Other shopping will become particular and personal – special clothes, special foods, the fruit, the fish that needs to be personally selected; and it will once more be bought in a small shop with dialogue between seller and customer. We may well seek out theatre in exactly the same way. It will be the entertainment that is special because it insists that we participate and use our imaginations. And we shall find it very special because it is live. We affect the performance and it affects us. The result is slightly different every night and that difference is its strength: it is always different because it is alive. So let us celebrate that it is elitist. Standards usually are.

In the age of Shakespeare, the British made the greatest theatre culture in history. It was a clear demonstration of their genius for creation. But within thirty years, their genius for destruction (which is often quite as pervasive) had obliterated the entire achievement. A great tradition was destroyed. Perhaps it is the tension of the British temperament between Cavalier eccentricity and Roundhead control which makes us subject to these puritanical fits of disapproval. Intense passions near to madness war with guilty restraint; eccentricity and originality fight with restraining dogma. It certainly makes us love art and hate art in equal measure. We are often proud of being philistine, and we are the only country in Europe who uses "intellectual" as a term of abuse. These neurotic swings of mood from the pragmatic to the mechanistic, the Dionysian to the Apollonian, are particularly British. They may be why we are so particularly good at making theatre. It is also why governments have spent the last twenty years indifferently destroying what was by any reckoning a golden age of theatre. The destruction still continues.

We create in pleasure and repent in pain. We destroy what we create with self-righteous enthusiasm

– particularly if we feel guilty because of the joy we have found in the creation. Or if it costs money. We invent, but we do not conserve. So art – and particularly theatre – is something we prefer to undervalue and it is always under threat. In this we are proud to be unlike the French.

Let us therefore reiterate: the stage is art. It is a social art which at its best challenges and provokes at the same instant that it entertains. It is performance art, it is not literature. It must be studied with a sense of performance even when it is read. I believe that to study a play text is a specialised skill, as specialised as learning to read a score of music. We can all read, and therefore we think we can all evaluate literature. But we need to learn the language of the theatre if we are to judge drama, just as we need to understand musical forms if we are to study opera. We must develop knowledge and skills which take us beyond reading texts just as texts. A script of a play is only the verbal plan of the event, not the event itself. Drama begins with form. And that is what we need to study if we are to understand drama. Form is a mask which exposes as it hides. It is never – ever – real. If it is successful, it persuades us that it represents the real.

There is a story about Chekhov and Stanislavsky. Chekhov was told that Stanislavsky intended to have frogs croaking, the sound of dragonflies, and dogs barking on the stage. "Why?" Chekhov asked with a note of dissatisfaction in his voice. "It is realistic" he was told. "Realistic", Chekhov repeated with a laugh, and after a slight pause he said: "The stage is art. There is a canvas of Kramskoi (who was a famous Russian painter) in which he wonderfully depicts human faces. Suppose he eliminated the nose of one of these faces and substituted a real one. The nose would certainly be real, but the picture would be spoiled."